An American Café
Reflections From The Grill

by

Peter C. Gianakura

Take time to reflect!
Warm Wishes

Peter C. Gianakura

ABOUT THE AUTHOR

Peter Gianakura was born and raised in Sault Ste. Marie, Michigan. He graduated in 1940 from Sault High School and attended Cleary College. He served in the U.S. Army Medical Corps for over four years during World War II, after which he attended Sault Tech, now Lake Superior State University, when it was established in Sault Ste. Marie. Peter owned and operated The American Café, a family business for over 43 years. He is married to Georgia, and they are the parents of three daughters and have six grandchildren.

This book is dedicated to our customers,
with endless thanks for their patronage
and the memories they left.

Tales from the Table

Our Papa would come home from work every evening with a cheerful whistle announcing his arrival. We would drop whatever we were doing and run to the back door shouting, "Papa's home, Papa's home!" After he gathered his kisses from his daughters, he would sit peacefully for the first time that day and eat his dinner at the special seat always reserved for him— pre-set awaiting his arrival. Most days we had already eaten our dinner, but we would join him at the table and wait with anticipation for "the list". "The list" was a small piece of paper which would peak out of our Papa's shirt pocket that was filled with special anecdotes, stories and ideas that filled his day. He would begin his meal, pull out "the list" and deliver a delicious array of stories. Each one made you hungrier for more.

Although he rarely cooked for us at home, he never failed to serve up a great story. Our bellies were always filled with fantastic concoctions from our Mama's magical dinners, and our hearts and minds were filled with our Papa's wonderful stories. Our kitchen table was the heart of our home, vibrant with meals and conversation, and we grew up knowing we were loved.

That kitchen table continues to serve up the same love and care that was shared long ago when we were young, and our children are now blessed by the experience. The stories are always fresh and the food outstanding!

If I had just one wish it would be that every child would have that same experience—a table abundant with a buffet of unconditional love, laughter, patience, story-telling and a great meal, too!

I'm so glad our Papa wrote down some of those stories from "the list". Welcome to our kitchen table . . .

– Anastasia Gianakura Stacey

Foreword

A while back I was rummaging through a desk drawer looking for something or other when I came across a copy of the official coat of arms of the "Sowhatwhocares Club." It consisted of a drawing of a three-toed sloth and a service club emblem with a slash through it. Across the top was the legend Quis Curat? (To readers with Latin knowledge, forgive any mistake as I am reconstructing this from memory; the actual document having settled back into the detritus.) The club had no officers, no constitution, no bylaws and only one hard and fast rule: "Don't get carried away on your hobbyhorse because you'll bore the hell out of the rest of us." It began, to the best of my memory, because certain people in our morning coffee group went on at too great length about certain subjects: politics, their golf game, last night's basketball game, that sort of thing. They were, in other words, too engaged. They CARED TOO MUCH. Certainly they cared more than anyone listening to them. One of our group, Tom Ewing, even constructed a device for shushing these monologists. It consisted of a bell and a horn mounted on a little stand and when someone broke the rule, the device was activated to shut them up.

I don't know what happened to this curious artifact. Peter probably disposed of it when he sold the restaurant. He had kept it carefully stored behind the counter, to be dragged out when we came in, along with the extension allowing us to expand the seating area around the booth that we normally occupied in The American Café. I think Peter enjoyed this nonsense, as he enjoyed so much that went on in that place, hard as the work may have been. The American was a special place, a part of Americana that is probably disappearing, even from small towns. The "Sowhatwhocares" meetings took place thirty years or so ago when there was a more vital downtown. The space is now occupied along with the other store fronts and the movie theatre by a struggling but determined group of people who have started a performing arts school and performance theatre, which is thriving against all odds. Long may it live and prosper!

The American Café is long gone but not forgotten, least of all by Peter, who thankfully has a great memory and a great ability to get the memories on paper. His memories are poignant, especially when they tell of a young man who really very much wanted to do something else, but like many of us in this life, found that fate had something quite different in store. The memories are very tender and warm when he speaks of the wonderful family that helped him in this enterprise. And above all the memories are very funny. There are lots of goofy people out there and an inordinate number of them seem to have wandered into The American at one time or another. With wry affection, Peter has evoked them. While he was seemingly absorbed in the business of frying hamburgers, he was also always observing and not much was lost on him.

When I moved to Sault Ste. Marie in 1974 to manage the jewelry store down the street from The American, I of course went there for coffee and lunch. Everybody did. You had to wait for seats at lunch time. It was good fare, reasonably priced. Great burgers. Great chili. The place had its own ambience, a permanent smell of fried onions and cigarette smoke in those days when no one thought of forbidding smoking anywhere. Around ten or so in the morning, there would be the smell of burnt toast. That didn't signal carelessness at the toaster. It meant that Peter finally was able to sit down and read the Free Press and have a cup of coffee and toast the way he liked it—cremated.

There was a sign over the mirror behind the counter: YOU ARE A STRANGER HERE BUT ONCE. I know, anybody can put up a sign like that and you see them everywhere. This one, however, I think was true. When I first went into the café and met Peter our conversation quickly revealed a shared taste for classical music. The next time I went in, he turned off whatever was on the radio and popped a tape of Mozart into the player. It was that kind of place. I still miss it.

– Leon Bennett

TABLE OF CONTENTS

The Laying to Rest of Ghosts

A Celebration of Living

"Autobiography can be the laying to rest of ghosts as well as an ordering of the mind. But for me, it is also a celebration of living and an attempt to hoard its sensations."

— *Laurie Lee, I Can't Stay Long*

The Laying to Rest of Ghosts

In the Beginning—Prologue

What I remember about those early days is what my father told me. This came in bits and pieces over the years. When one is young, matters of the past mean nothing. It is the now, the present that is important. Not until we become older do we begin to question the how and why of the past—if at all. Then, in many cases, it is too late. Our source dies and we find ourselves regretting the passage of time and not being inquisitive enough.

My father and uncle, as well as millions of other immigrants, came to this great country totally unprepared for the adjustments and adaptations they would have to make. The language barrier must have been a challenge itself—trying to communicate by making themselves understood and to understand others, learning the various denominations of money, coping with customs and manners and acclimating to the culture of food as opposed to the foods to which they were accustomed in their own countries. There was so much to absorb, it must have been overwhelming.

They survived, contributed, and added to the growth and development of a great, free nation. For many their spirit and determination was expressed in becoming entrepreneurs. They had a pioneering spirit, and America was fertile ground for them.

What I have just written has been addressed in great detail and studied by historians and social scientists, yet I feel it necessary to expound briefly on this immigrant picture since it involved my father and uncle and, inevitably, The American Café.

A Short History

Just why my father and my Uncle Sam came to Sault Ste. Marie, Michigan, (the Soo) in 1900 is something that remains a mystery. Perhaps I was told ever so many years ago, but being young it didn't mean much to me at the time. In the late 1800s, America was a dream with its "streets paved in gold and money hanging from trees." On their arrival reality hit them, and I'm sure it was a hard reality. So many Greek immigrants settled along the eastern shores of America. New York, Long Island, Boston all became populated with immigrants from all nations. Ethnic neighborhoods were created in many of these communities. But why Michigan? Why Sault Ste. Marie? At about that time, the local tannery was in full production and Union Carbide was hiring. Most of the employees were immigrants from Finland, Italy, Slovakian countries, Poland and Greece. Perhaps someone from Greece made it known that the Soo was an area of opportunity.

As time passed, my father and my Uncle Sam found the jobs they had at the tannery were becoming too routine. One day, as they walked down Portage Avenue and at the corner of Magazine Street, they saw a small vacant building for rent. Across the street was the railroad depot. The train was just about the only means of transportation in and out of the Soo for the majority of the population during those years. They observed the activity in and around the train station. People coming and going brought to mind that travelers were in need of items—candy, gum, tobacco, newspapers. The brothers felt they had everything to gain and nothing to lose, considering they came to their newly adopted country with just a small suitcase and a determination to establish themselves as productive citizens. Entrepreneurship was in their blood, and America was the place. They rented the vacant building. (It was at one time a fact that many Greek immigrants to America eventually owned and operated their own restaurants, candy stores and ice cream

2

parlors. Why this came about, I can only speculate. Perhaps on arriving in this land, totally foreign to them, they found work in such places as dishwashers, custodians and cooks. With a driving ambition to learn and succeed in their newly adopted country, they expanded upon what they initially learned.)

My father and uncle had barely enough capital to furnish their new enterprise with merchandise. In order to make an impression that they were well stocked with supplies, they filled the shelves on the wall facing the customers with boxes. The emblem that identified their new enterprise and conveyed respect and love for their adopted country was a golden eagle with wings outspread as if in flight was painted on their storefront window. This little place was their beginning in the world of free enterprise in a free country. The enterprise moved nine times over the years, and at one point the brothers had two businesses going simultaneously. The nine locations brought them closer and closer to the spreading business community which in its final phase became known as The American Café, in the center of town, on Ashmun Street.

Homemade candy was most popular at the turn of the 20th century. Offering sweet delicacies in one's shop was a profitable attraction. My Uncle Sam and my father decided they should add this feature to their small establishment. My uncle went to Chicago, where he learned the fine art of making candy—chocolates of all descriptions and fillings, toffees and peanut brittles.

On Sam's return to the Soo, the brothers bought the necessary equipment to produce homemade candy products. This included large copper kettles with round bottoms; large gas stoves; steel hooks attached to posts which were used for pulling toffee; large, thick slabs of marble, and all kinds of wooden paddles with spoons almost as large as shovels.

The brothers also began to make ice cream. I remember they called it Velvet ice cream because it was so smooth and rich. Farmers brought milk and cream to their confectionary in five-gallon, galvanized metal containers. There were endless bottles, all brown, that contained food coloring and flavorings of all sorts.

The ice cream was sold on the premises in sodas, sundaes, floats, malted milks and milkshakes. When the ice cream cone was introduced in the Soo at the shop, people would lick the ice cream out of the cone and throw the cone away. My father and uncle had to teach them that the cone was edible. Ice cream to take home was hand-packed. When it was offered for sale as pre-packaged, the pints and quarts were filled directly from the ice cream maker when the ice cream was still soft. With this method, the ice cream was sold at a much lower price. When the ice cream was sold hand-packed, it cost more.

I remember seeing my uncle exert tremendous energy, gleaming with sweat while he used huge wooden paddles, mixing candy ingredients in a large copper kettle as it was heated by the gas stove. He would stir the contents until they began to bubble. At one point he would place a thermometer in the kettle, grunt with approval and turn off the stove. After a while, he would pick the material up in his bare hands, throw it over a large metal hook and begin pulling it strand by strand with great effort until he felt it was ready to be unhooked. He would then spread it on a marble slab into sheets one to two inches thick. After it cooled to a certain temperature, he would take a large, sharp knife, and cut long strips of it, and then cut these into pieces of one or two inches. When cooled entirely and hardened, the toffee would be bagged, weighed and sold. This was toffee of different colors and flavors. I was about five years old at the time and very fascinated. (A memento of these days is a smaller marble slab that we now use as the top of our wooden desk. Today it serves as a surface for writing, but, oh, the aromas and sweets that come to mind when I touch it are as vivid as those years ago.)

A similar process created the peanut brittle. Instead of pulling it on the hook, my uncle picked up the huge copper kettle and poured its contents onto the marble slab when the peanut mixture reached a certain temperature. You could see it very slowly spread. Its consistency meant that it always spread to a desired thickness, and there it would be left to cool. After the candy hardened, my uncle picked up a small, shiny chrome-plated hammer, and struck the mixture in various spots. The peanut brittle shattered into pieces. These would be placed in bags, weighed and priced.

One day I watched this process. After pouring the mixture, Uncle Sam turned to me and warned me not to touch the hot candy. I could burn myself. Of course, when he turned away, I stuck my fingers into this molten mass and immediately felt great pain.

All of the chocolates had a special design or insignia identifying the type of filling they contained. On learning the trademark, one could tell whether the contents were cream, cherry cordial, nougat or caramel centers. It all took a practiced hand. This candy-making arena was my Uncle Sam's domain, while my father took care of the restaurant upstairs.

One great feature of candy making was the creative variety of candy canes for the Christmas season. These ranged from small, finger-sized canes, to some as tall as a regular walking cane. They were flavored with peppermint or wintergreen.

My Uncle Sam died from stomach cancer in 1927. He suffered terribly. A lengthy stay at Johns Hopkins Medical Center was not helpful. My father could not handle the double duty of processing candy and ice cream at the same time as managing the beverage and food establishment. So, in 1932 when the Greek community built its first church after renting a small building for several years, my father donated the large marble slab, used for candy-making, to be used as the altar. This huge piece was close to six inches thick, four feet wide, and six feet long. It served its Holy purpose until 1947 when a fire caused severe damage to the interior of the church. The heat was so intense that it shattered the marble slab into gravel-like pieces.

The remainder of the candy processing equipment remained idle for many years, until World War II. When our country became involved and scrap metal was needed for the war effort, my father donated the copper kettles, stoves and other equipment to his adopted country.

It seems a paradox that apparatus used for processing sweet delicacies became part of a church and were put to use in fighting a war. I believe my Uncle Sam would have approved of how it all turned out.

5

In the early years our establishment was called the "American Ice Cream Parlor and Confectionary." An advertisement from a 1911 edition of The Evening News, Sault Ste. Marie's local paper, yellow with age and somewhat fragile, indicates two establishments—one for Christmas candies and fruit called "The American Confectionary," and the other, the restaurant, was called "The London."

This newspaper advertisement from *The Evening News*, December 18, 1911, shows my father and his brother had the two businesses at the same time.

One of the last locations of the business was on Ashmun Street, three doors down from the corner of Ashmun and Spruce Streets. The café was there for a good 25 years and would have been there much longer if it had not been for the arrival of a chain store. One day my father noticed a man standing on one of the street corners. In his hand he had an instrument that he seemed to be playing with. This went on for two or three days.

6

My father, curious, approached the man, and asked him what he was doing. He was counting pedestrian traffic at that point of the city, since it was the heart of the downtown business section. Some months went by and my father was sent an eviction notice. He had to move because that whole area was purchased by the Kresge Company, and they were to put in a new establishment.

About that time, a new structure was being erected just up the street in the same block. This was to house a movie theatre and four small businesses. This was a fortunate happening since all my father had to do was move several stores south on the same block. This happened in 1930. The American Café remained there through my ownership of it until 1989.

When my father took over the new location, he requested two stores instead of one. Doing so allowed an opening to be made in the wall as an entrance to the second store. This area housed brand new booths for dining. The main entrance had the ice cream fountain and kitchen. On the opposite wall homemade candies were on display.

Although everything fell into place, considering the eviction and the availability of the new location, it was a bad time for business. The Great Depression had hit the country, and the Soo was no exception. I've read, and heard, that the Soo was not hit as hard as other parts of the country, yet my father found it difficult to raise five of us while paying rent for two store spaces. The customers were not indulging in handmade chocolate delicacies. My father was no longer able to make his own ice cream, so he purchased it from the local dairy. He fell behind with his rent and his ice cream purchases.

One Depression-era memory from the café is very vivid to me. Occasionally, a man came in and sitting at the counter, he softly, embarrassingly and humbly asked the waitress if he could have a cup of hot water. On receiving it, he would reach for the catsup; pour some in his cup of hot water, stir and drink. Perhaps this was the only nourishment he had had for quite some time. This occurred several times with different men. My father, on learning this, instructed the girls to also give them crackers or bread or even overlook the request for hot water and

7

give them soup and a sandwich. Unemployment had caused such dire straits, and I couldn't help but think how depressing such circumstances must be to those without work.

I recall that Mr. Charles Chipley approached my father to collect the rent. They sat and talked for quite a while. Mr. Chipley was the agent who took care of the building's needs, collecting rent and managing the facilities. He was in real estate. He was a tall, slender man, always dressed immaculately in gray conservative suits. He smoked cigarettes on a long holder. He was serious and businesslike, and he expressed his regret that my father might have to move or lose his business because of his delinquent rent payments. They decided that my father could survive if he gave up the dining area, covered the newer entrance, and squeezed the café into just one of the stores. This meant the long candy display case had to go. The twelve booths in the dining area were to be moved to where the candy counter once stood, but the space could only accommodate seven booths. The remaining five were sold to a tavern. This "downsizing" helped the café survive this difficult time, because the rent was cut in half.

The ice cream debt was reduced considerably by having my father pay double the amount for five-gallon containers. Of course, this cut down his profit considerably. In time, he caught up with his debt. Mr. George Geirbach, the owner/manager of the Soo Creamery, was most considerate and sympathetic of my father's financial dilemma. He and Mr. Chipley were, in my mind, kind businessmen. We were fortunate to have had these men in charge at a time of need.

My Father

My father was an energetic man, industrious and untiring. For many years he worked seven days a week, twelve to fourteen hours a day. He was short, about 5'5", stocky, but not hefty, and he walked as if the devil were chasing him. When we walked together, I almost had to run to keep up with him. Whether this was a natural inherited quality or whether it became a part of him because of the nature of his work, I never knew. A restaurant operator is a damnably demanding occupation. There is always something to be attended to, from seeing to the needs of the customer to the preparation of the necessary foods and beverages to the dispensing of the same. There is no dilly-dallying. You are always at the beck and call of the customer in every respect. If this part of the business is neglected then one's success is in jeopardy. My father's total commitment and preoccupation with his work was such that I never really got to know him until I was put into service at the café at about the age of 12. The fathers of my schoolmates made time to go fishing with their sons, hunt with them, play catch, go to a movie, go on a picnic—all the wonderful activities that create a bond and make lasting memories. I reflect on this at times and I often wonder if I ever truly had a "childhood." My father was also put to work at quite a young age so I assume he, too, was deprived of his youth. This was a way of life for him. He knew nothing else but a strong work ethic.

My father and my Uncle Sam were determined to be successful in their new country and perpetual hard work was one way of doing it. What added to their determination was that they loved it. This single-mindedness in trying to achieve their piece of the American Dream, plus their work ethic, was ingrained in them. They were so obsessed with reaching their goal that nothing else mattered. They never developed outside interests or hobbies. Their business ventures were their entire life.

Besides his passion for his business, my father was a religious man. He followed the tenets of the Greek Orthodox Church with total devotion. There was no formal church structure in the Soo, no priest. If a sacramental event, such as a funeral, wedding or baptism came along, a priest would come up from Detroit or Chicago, perform the sacred rites and leave. As the male immigrants married and offspring came into the picture, the fathers realized if they were to maintain their Greek heritage and ensure such with their children, it was going to

9

be necessary to find a full-time priest to care for their spiritual and cultural needs. Eventually a priest was hired, but still having no church building, various halls were rented for such a purpose. The Greek immigrants were a hot-tempered lot and politically were still involved with what was going on in their native Greece. If the hired priest did not live up to their expectations politically, then he would be released, and they would seek another one. My father was a monarchist and he seemed to be in the minority among his fellow Greeks, but he never made this a criterion when it came to the spiritual aspects of his life. His church was the center of life followed by his culture and providing for his family.

New Booths

As a young boy, it was difficult to pronounce my last name, "Gianakura," (pronounced with a hard "g" and a silent "i"—"ganakura"). The café provided me with an easier to vocalize "last name" that I used in answer to the question, "What's your name, little boy?" I would respond with, "Peter Coca-Cola". It would often raise a smile and a chuckle.

When the café moved to its final location on Ashmun Street next to the movie theatre, I witnessed the assembly of the new booths by carpenters. I recall standing nearby, watching with the fascination that a youngster of seven or eight years of age is prone to have.

As I stood there, I recall one of our customers beside me, observing the activity as I was. After a few minutes he tapped me gently on the head and said, "Peetair, are you cleaningk your diningk room?" With that said, he walked away.

I was surprised, as well as puzzled, by his remark and could not imagine what he was talking about. Then it occurred to me that in my rapt attention to the carpenters at work, I was also poking my finger in my nostrils. A nasty habit that, I'm sure, just about every youngster has at some time or another.

The observer of my nasty habit was August Stelter. August was an immigrant from Germany. He was a slight man and an expert tailor. Many times I saw him in his little tailor shop, sitting on the table with his legs crossed before him, diligently and expertly stitching and altering clothes.

August was an avid coffee drinker. He always poured his coffee from his cup into his saucer. Carefully, expertly, he would drink his coffee from the saucer. Even when there were hot, humid days during the summer, August still had hot coffee. Everyone else insisted on a cold beer or soda drink. Not August. He claimed that drinking hot coffee under such conditions cooled a person better than a cold drink. He smoked incessantly and did so with great relish. One could tell he enjoyed the whole process, from the first puff, to the last. He smoked non-filtered Camels until he died in his late nineties.

Grasshoppers

One hot summer day when I had no immediate obligation at The American Café, I noticed that the number of grasshoppers in the neighborhood had grown tremendously. I was bored, sitting on the front porch steps, trying to drum up some adventure. My neighborhood playmate was away, and I had no one else to play with.

In the meantime, the grasshoppers were having a field day. As I stared at their activity I wondered if I could catch some of them. I ran into the basement, found a large, empty pickling jar, and back outdoors I went. It did not take long for me to fill the jar to the top with the insects. Now, what to do with them? I just had to show off my latest conquest to someone.

I remembered one of my favorite waitresses was working, so I walked excitedly to the café to show her my loot. This was in the middle of summer. Tourism was at its peak. The café was jammed with customers. As I entered the café I noticed my waitress friend was behind the counter, busy making a couple of banana splits. She was just topping off the sundae with whipped cream.

She was truly concentrating on her creation when I excitedly told her about the grasshoppers. Breathlessly I asked her if she would like to see them. She said "Yes."

I immediately, unthinkingly and excitedly unscrewed the top, removed it, and in a split second the captured grasshoppers found their freedom and began hopping all over the ice cream, the counter and throughout the restaurant. The waitresses screamed, the customers yelled, and pandemonium ensued.

I grabbed my jar and ran home. That night I felt the sting of the rubber hose my father always seemed to have handy. He must have had two of them – one at the house, and one at the café. They both had the same result: humiliation, pain, and tears.

Summertime

It was early morning and two of the boys in our neighborhood came by to play. One of our favorite haunts was the alley running behind our house between Carrie Street and Dawson Street. This was the site of fun and imagination. There were lots of places to hide and play "cops and robbers," "cowboys and Indians," and "hide and seek"—games most suitable for our energetic bodies and fertile imaginations. We were in the process of one of our games, and I heard my mother calling me from the back door. I found a moment to respond, and she told me my father had called and wanted me to hurry and get to the café. I was having too much fun to go obediently so back to fun I went. Sometime later, my mother called again and I responded with some non-committal reply. This went on three to four times, but I kept on having my fun.

In the heat of our play, I hid behind our neighbor's garage

waiting for the next maneuver by my playmates. Suddenly I heard my name called by one of them, and I stepped out of my hiding place and out to the alley. As I looked up, I saw my father coming toward me with his apron on and a mean and determined look on his face. I was paralyzed with surprise and fright and didn't budge. I stood there until he first grabbed my arm and then pulled me down the alley by my ear toward the store. How long he held my ear and pulled me along I don't recall, but I do know we reached the store and I was put to work—mainly washing dishes and cleaning tables. Gone was my fun in the sun. This was not an isolated incident. Many times I wonder where my youth went. I certainly did not participate in most of the activities of my peers. They seemed to have a freedom that I envied but could never fully share.

Many times during the summer as I puttered around the store, I'd hear a tap, tap on the window or a waitress would bring to my attention some of my friends who were outside. I'd look up and they would be waving their swimming trunks and towels and pointing to the west. This of course indicated they were going swimming. Sometimes one of the bolder ones would come in and invite me to go. I could never just leave; I'd ask my father and point to the gang waiting, and his answer was always a definite "No."

One day, somehow, I managed to find some time with the guys, my only time with them at the swimming hole. Never having had the freedom to explore my surroundings, I was totally intrigued by their familiarity with the nooks and corners of our town. The swimming hole was at the head of the Locks back in a shallow, private area reached by a small, narrow tree-lined path. Suddenly there appeared the St. Marys River. This area was a shallow inlet in a wooded area called "The Jungle." On arriving there, I realized I had no swimming trunks. The rest of the fellows had theirs. On mentioning this, we all decided we would go in the buff. At first I was reluctant, fearing that we would be seen. I was assured that no one was ever present and we all should be free to have fun. The water was quite warm, and I realized why they called this swimming hole the "piss pot." I also soon realized I couldn't swim worth a fig.

13

My fellow companions swam like fish—daring and carefree. I envied them.

I did not learn to swim until I was a senior in high school, because swimming the length of the high school pool was a graduation requirement. Any swimming I have done since has been just that—the usual length of a pool, and after that I'm exhausted. This lack of freedom as a child and young man, being on an invisible tether, has always been a thorn in my side, and I can't help but feel it had a bearing on my lack of a spirit of adventure—always cautious, analyzing pros and cons and getting lost in a maze of "should I or shouldn't I?" In fact, when I entered the army and was stationed in Seattle, over 2,000 miles away from home, I'd find myself asking, "What would my father say?" Whenever I was given a 24-hour pass or weekend pass, I wondered what he would say if he knew I went to the Seattle Zoo or attended a Russian Orthodox Church instead of a Greek Orthodox Church. His "hold" on me was powerful.

The Fall

During the Great Depression in the 1930's, my father found it hard to feed and clothe five growing youngsters, and I'm sure he had many trying days full of worry and concern. One fine day when I arrived at the store after school to allow my father a chance to go home to have supper, rest, and return, he was unpacking a huge crate. When all was finished, there stood a brand new sparkling popcorn machine. From early spring until late fall the popcorn stand was irresistible to pedestrians. The popcorn stand became a family affair. During the summers, my father taught my sisters the ins and outs of running this new enterprise. When school ended for the season, each of my sisters took turns at the stand. The aroma of fresh popcorn and our proximity to the theatre made a natural magnet for theatre-bound customers. Many people passing by on other business would stop for popcorn.

About this time, I felt a growing sense of adventure—I was entering junior high. My new school was just across the street from where we lived. I was told that we moved from classroom to classroom for each subject, instead of being in one room all day, and I was ready! About a week after school started my enthusiasm came to a screeching halt. Tragedy struck.

Each day in the late morning, my father pulled the popcorn stand out of the café and placed it on the edge of the sidewalk, next to the café entrance. The electrical cord to the popcorn stand was fed through a small hole at the base of the café entrance. This cord was then plugged into the electrical outlet in the ceiling of the basement. On one particular day, however, the stand was not getting the electric power it required. My father went to the basement and discovered the plug was dangling and not inserted into the outlet. Being short in stature he stood on a box to reach up and reinsert the plug, but the box was not as sturdy as he thought. One minute he was on the box, the next minute he was on the floor.

He was taken to the hospital where x-rays revealed a fractured thigh bone. The procedure for fixing the break necessitated the insertion of a metal plate and screws, and a lengthy stay in the hospital followed by recuperation time at home. Who was to run the café? The responsibility fell to me. In my limited capacity I had to do the best I could, which meant leaving school and replacing my father. How I managed I do not remember, except for some trying and emotional moments. I was 12 years old.

We were open on Sundays then. I remember a customer coming in for a hot pork sandwich. He came quite early, way before noon. I wanted to accommodate him, so I quickly managed to put things together. I remember my father always had extra gravy made. All I needed to do was heat it. I reached into the fridge, pulled out a container, poured it in a pan, and in a short time assembled his hot pork sandwich. He began to eat it. After a mouthful or two, he called me over to try it out. I did and found the gravy to be sickeningly sweet. I checked its source and discovered it wasn't gravy I had heated, but butterscotch for ice cream sundaes. The color and consistency were

15

very much the same. The man settled for a hamburger.

Another time I forgot to light the gas-operated steam table. The mashed potatoes were cold until this was brought to my attention. I wept with frustration and a sense of helplessness.

After a few days went by, in came Mr. Taylor. He was the truant officer from the school system. I explained to him what had happened. He was sympathetic but told me that something had to be done to get me back in school. Not long after, an itinerant Greek cook came to the rescue. He took over at the Café until my father was able to get back to work. I gratefully returned to school. This was an unforgettable experience and, for a 12 year old boy, a traumatic one.

LIFE

As we grow up, many of us find a hero, someone we admire and wish to emulate. In high school in the late 1930's, I was taking journalism and developed a liking for photography. Along came LIFE magazine. Here was a publication that reflected the old axiom, "a picture is worth a thousand words."

About that time the Russo-Finnish war was going on. Battles were being fought in sub-zero weather. LIFE sent Karl Mydans to cover the war being waged under these miserable, cold conditions. The shutters in his cameras would freeze, so he found it necessary to keep one camera next to his body to keep the camera shutters free to operate, and he would alternate cameras. In addition to his photographs, he reported on the war. Up to this point in the journalism world an assignment was given to a reporter and, depending on the story, a photographer would also be assigned. With Karl Mydans, along came the "photojournalist", a two-in-one career. On reading about him, his challenges and accomplishments, Karl Mydans became my hero.

When I told my father about my new fascination and aspiration, he painted a bitter picture. These people, he said, had no home, no base. They were always at the beck and call of an assignment and never settled anywhere. He pronounced that it would be no life for a man who may marry and have a family and certainly no life for his son. Because these words were uttered by my father, my enthusiasm was dampened and my dream shattered.

Man's Folly

I worked in The American Café until the Japanese attack on Pearl Harbor. Some months later I tried to enlist in the Coast Guard, and then the Air Force, but my flawed vision did not meet their requirements. I waited and worked in the restaurant until the one fine day the draft came along. I received my notice that the U.S. Army would accept me in spite of my visual limitations, so on November 11, Armistice Day, I went for a physical in Marquette, Michigan. There were dozens of us standing in line, naked, examined by doctors one after the other. Suddenly a command demanded our attention. We all stood still and from one end of the gym came the soulful taps. How ironic, I thought: We were acknowledging the end of World War I, the "war to end all wars", and commemorating the dead of that war on this Armistice Day as we stood, stark naked, being prepared for another fling at man's folly.

In My Absence

Because of my absence from The American Café during World War II, I was not fully aware of how the café was coping with the sudden influx of U.S. Army personnel to Sault Ste. Marie. In spite of its seemly remote geographic location, the Soo was a key strategic site to be defended because of the

17

Locks, which allowed iron ore and grain for the war effort to be shipped from the upper Midwest to the industrial cities of Chicago, Detroit and Cleveland. The Army had a large base on the property that later became Lake Superior State University. My sister, Helen Gianakura Reinkensmeyer, does remember and she writes . . .

If you were looking for my father and did not find him in church or at home, he was working at The American Café. He routinely opened the café before 7 a.m. to have the coffee ready for the workers from J.C. Penney's and Montgomery Ward. His day went on until after the "late show", the second movie next door at the Soo Theatre was over at around 11 p.m.—still hoping for some hungry customers. My sister, Sophie, and I felt it just wasn't worth the wait, but to my father every penny counted. When we were small, we rarely saw our father, being gone all day as he was. But I knew when he came home late at night. I could hear him wearily climbing the steps, stopping at our bedroom door, checking on us and dropping some coins in our fruit juice cans which he had made into piggy banks. I could smell him, too. He smelled of smoke and French fries. Faithful mother would be in bed with her bed light on, reading and waiting for him.

Before the war, the number of café customers increased in June as tourists, along with hay fever sufferers taking advantage of the clear air, arrived in town. After Labor Day there was a quiet spell until the deer hunters descended upon the town. Once they left, it was quiet again until Christmas shoppers stopped for lunch and refreshment. The income and savings for maintaining the family were primarily gathered from June to December and had to be meted out frugally to get us through the winter months. Expenses were high during the winter, what with having to pay for tons of coal used to fuel the furnace. Along with that went winter clothes for four growing children.

With the war in full swing, Peter in the service and hundreds of GIs coming to The American Café for a meal or a beer, my father slaved in the hot kitchen with no air conditioning while my sister Sophie and I worked long hours waiting on tables. Since I was only 15 years old, my father had to get special permission for me to serve beer. Even then, I could not serve beer to customers seated in the booths, only at the counter.

Sophie and I were in charge of popping and selling popcorn. Father would roll the popcorn stand out in front of the store. While Sophie and I popped, our brother, Sammy, and baby sister, Joy, helped make boxes for the popcorn. It was a family affair. We worked hard and to quote father, "we worked together as a team."

Opportunities Missed

I am quite sure opportunities come to many people in various ways. Some are overlooked, some are investigated and action or inaction occurs depending on the individual's disposition, inclination or circumstances.

I was on the train on my way home with my discharge papers in my pocket, and wondering what I was going to do once I got there. Over four years had passed since I left the Soo, and during that time I had not given any serious thought to my future. Sitting opposite me on the train was a pleasant couple. The man was dressed in a suit and had a friendly and professional look about him. Through our conversation I discovered he was on the faculty of a small liberal arts school, St. Olaf College in Northfield, Minnesota. He told me of the G. I. Bill that would be offered to veterans and suggested that I look into it. We parted as he and his wife changed trains for the west, and I continued north to the Soo. Before he left he gave me his card and told me to contact him if I should decide to attend St. Olaf. He said he would be most happy to help me in any way. I never contacted him. An opportunity missed.

A year or more after my discharge, I found myself once again quite involved in the café just as I had been before I left. My father was 73 at the time, and no amount of pleading from anyone could persuade him to retire. His stock answer was always, "If you want me to die quickly, retirement would do it. I must work." So he and I plodded along—my sisters and brother having moved on to other interests.

One of our steady customers was a tall, well-dressed man.

He would sit at the counter and have coffee and a Danish. Once in a while, when I had a moment, we would chat. One day he asked me if I would be interested in working with him. I noticed he said working "with him" instead of "for him." Up to that point I had no idea what he did. I was impressed by the man. He was mannerly and pleasant, and he reminded me of the movie stars Gary Cooper and Randolph Scott—quiet, confident, determined. He had been a pilot in the U.S. Air Force during World War II and was discharged about the same time as I was. On returning to civilian life, he decided to sell insurance. He represented the Lincoln National Life Insurance Company as their sole representative in the area. He told me the time and the area was ripe for selling life insurance. Young men were returning to civilian life from the war. They were getting married, having families, and their need for insurance was great. He said he never realized the opportunities in this field, or the great potential, until he became involved in making them available as an agent. He needed help because it was overwhelming and he asked if I would consider becoming an insurance salesman. The company would train me, and I would be assigned to work with him. It all sounded most tempting. I told him I would think about it.

As I reflect on that opportunity and recall the impact that insurance was to have at that time, I remember that the Prudential Life Insurance Company and the Metropolitan Life Insurance Company had also opened offices in the Soo with as many as ten insurance agents handling the Eastern Upper Peninsula. And here was this man needing help and offering me the opportunity to provide it.

I also felt my 73 year old father needed help. He was industrious, dedicated to his café, but it appeared he had lost a certain zest for "keeping up with the times". The floor in the café was worn and unsightly. The stools were a menace—high, awkward and some would say even dangerous. The café needed a facelift. As I concentrated on these conditions, the insurance opportunity faded away.

Joe Cunningham was two years ahead of me in high school. Everybody knew Joe. He was quite an extrovert and involved in just about every school activity. He had a steady, happy-go-lucky disposition. When World War II broke out, he was out of high school. Joe went away into some branch of the service. On his return he was hired by the local newspaper in its advertising department. In a short time he became the assistant to the advertising manager. Two years later the veteran, long-time manager passed away and Joe stepped into his shoes. Not long after that, he came to the café and told me he needed help in his department. He would like to have me join him. This came as a surprise to me, much as the insurance sales offer several months prior. My immediate thoughts were that I would not be confined within the four walls of the café. I'd be in and out, able to circulate in all kinds of activity and in various situations. But a sense of obligation prevented me from accepting the job at the paper. Another opportunity missed.

A young man of my age left for the Army in 1942, the same time I did. We met each other for the first time on the bus to Fort Sheridan located just outside of Chicago, Illinois. On our return to the Soo over four years later, he entered his family's business. This was a well-established and successful department store. He learned the retail business entirely. When his father and uncle passed away, he continued to prosper. A year or so after losing his relatives, he realized that he needed help and approached me. At one time we were co-chairmen for the Red Cross Drive, an annual event. Between the two of us we made a huge success of it. If I recall correctly, the only cost we created in completing the fund drive for that year was $25. The Red Cross people were amazed. We did work well together. He knew I was not the happiest person doing what I was doing. He thought I could be an assistant to his business, and he wanted me to take over the men's department of his store. This, too, never materialized; I declined it for the same reason as the other "missed opportunities".

I had come home thinking I'd give myself a couple of weeks to find a new direction and orient myself to a new life. Little did I dream that those two weeks would become 43 years. I had followed in my father's footsteps, and in so doing I ignored the pursuit of my own dreams and ambitions.

Life provides many moments that can redirect us should we choose. While I reflect on those moments—those "opportunities"—and at times consider how things "might have been", I fully acknowledge that had I taken one of those roads, the stories I lived, some written here, would not be known to me. Now that, indeed, would be an opportunity missed.

The Popcorn "Stand"

Just inside the café to the immediate left was a showcase displaying candy bars, gum, and Lifesavers. Patrons to the theatre would stop in, make their purchases of popcorn and other delectables, and then go into the theatre. Countless candy and gum customers would come in and ask for Hursley bars instead of Hershey. The gum was often referred to as Wigley, not Wrigley, at which point the customer was asked—"Spearmint, Juicy Fruit or Doublemint?"

Mr. Sather, the theatre manager, regularly stood in front of the theatre watching the patrons, hands clasped behind him, his glistening bald head reflecting the marquee lights. He became aware of the edible merchandise that was being brought into the Soo Theatre by the movie patrons. I'm sure the debris left on the floor of the theatre itself made an impact enough so that he realized he was missing a service that he could provide to the moviegoers directly.

In due time, the theatre lobby acquired its own candy stand, complete with popcorn and soft drink dispensers. This accommodation diminished and finally ended the large amounts of candy, gum, and popcorn sold by The American Café. Times had changed the pattern of public purchases, as they tend to do.

Years later, it was my duty to open the café in the morning and get things started. Day after day, I became increasingly aware that the first thing that met one's eye was the old popcorn stand at the back facing the door. It had seen a better day, weathered many a storm and had lost its luster. For that matter, it was no longer used. My siblings and I, as well as the café, had outgrown it and the theatre was now serving popcorn to its patrons so there was no call for it. There it sat, useless and taking up space most unattractively. Nearly obscured behind the old popcorn stand was a new juke box. It sparkled in bright chrome and glass of striking colors. The juke box, in all its colorful splendor, was hidden from the public eye until a customer came in, was seated and after some scrutiny discovered it. There were also coin slots at each booth for making selections. Why should this attractive machine be hidden? Why couldn't I reverse their position and make that end of the café brighter and more visually appealing? One fine morning, I switched them around. I was pleased and so were the waitresses and customers. When my father arrived later in the morning, I was anxious to see his reaction. He came in walked up to the juke box, stared briefly and walked away. He put on his apron and began to work without a word. I felt that perhaps he wasn't quite in favor of my redecorating, but I was pleased and so the day went by and nothing was said.

When I opened the café the next morning, I immediately saw that the popcorn stand was back in its place and the juke box was hidden once again. The evening before, when it got dark, I purposely walked back and forth in front of the store as well as across the street to see what my move had done, and I was pleased—the whole store glistened attractively. You can imagine my dismay when I saw that my father had undone my improvement. I immediately switched them around. Again, when he came to work, not a word was spoken between us regarding this matter. But, the next morning he made the switch. Again, I reversed it. This went on day after day for almost a full week, when one morning I began my ritual and the popcorn stand would not budge, whereas before it was an easy matter to roll it around on its wheels. I tugged and pushed and it still stood its ground. I finally looked beneath and saw that my father had hammered spikes into the floor and wired the wheels to them. I was fuming, but by the time he came to work, I had cooled off. When he arrived, he looked at me with a smile indicating what both of us knew—he had outsmarted me and had the last word. I never pursued the matter again and never brought the subject up, but fortunately, some young Greek fellow soon bought the popcorn stand, and, I guess, I finally had my way—not through sheer will but by some luck.

The Sign

"If he wrote it, he could get rid of it. He had gotten rid of many things by writing them."
                              – Nick Adams by Ernest Hemingway

One day upon entering the café, I saw my father talking with Emmett Schmidt. Emmett earned his living as a sign painter. I couldn't imagine what they were discussing but didn't give it much thought. Two days later as I opened the store for the day, I was astonished to see the results of Emmett's and my father's plot. Poor Emmett did what he was told. Across the back wall just below the ceiling was a sign well over a foot high and running the full width of the café, almost 20 feet. The sign was painted a bright yellow with red letters and said, "You Are Welcome." In the middle were two hands clasping each other as in a hand shake. The whole thing to me was garish and ugly—evoking a symbol of communism. I became incensed.

When my father came, I didn't hesitate to tell him what I thought of the sign he had installed without my knowledge. Angry words came pouring out of me. Without waiting for an answer or looking at him, I removed my apron and ran out of the store. I recall getting into the car and my next awareness was of a red stop sign. As I came to it, I suddenly wondered where I was and how I got there. I was in Cedarville, some 30 miles out of the Soo, and I couldn't remember one mile of my drive. I sat at that stop sign shaking and realizing how easily I could have gotten into an accident. My anger had overcome any sensibility. I returned home and didn't go into the café for two days. When I did go back to work the sign was gone, and neither my father nor I spoke of it, nor spoke to each other for some time.

My father had never been inclined toward communism. As I reflect on this, I am sure he thought his sign was a sign of hospitality. To this day, I cannot identify why I had such a dramatic reaction to the sign. We had worked so closely together for so many years and perhaps there were some unresolved and unspoken issues that triggered my emotions.

The Canceled Order

About twice a year a pleasant salesman from C.J. Hungerford Smith and Company would come to the café to get our order for the season. He represented a fine quality product for ice cream fountains—ice cream toppings such as marshmallow, hot fudge, butterscotch, caramel and fruit. My father and the salesman would sit in a booth and discuss the needs for the store. Early spring would call for certain seasonal needs and in late fall different items would be required. We gave the orders and within two weeks they would come by American Railway Express.

One late summer, our regular salesman came to the store. My father greeted him in his broken English as he pointed to me, "My son will give you the order this time." I was surprised but thrilled that I would be given this responsibility. I was familiar with our inventory and needs, so I sat with the salesman quite confidently, but still flattered that this responsibility was now mine. The man was not a high-pressure salesman; he was a true gentleman, and we transacted the business in a friendly manner. In the end we shook hands, and he told me the order would be in the store no later than two weeks. This was customary.

As the days went by, I began to look forward to the shipment. I used to enjoy cutting open the boxes and placing the shiny half-gallon glass containers on the shelf and lining up the #10 tins of hot fudge and other syrups in order. The two weeks came and went and no order arrived. Soon it was three weeks and still no order. I asked my father if perchance the order came when I was out. He said, "No, there must be some reason for the delay—maybe they were very busy and couldn't keep up with the orders." A month passed, and I was truly concerned. About every other day I would call the American Railway Express for any information about the billing. The answer was always, "No." Five weeks passed, and I asked my father what could have happened to the order I had given the salesman. I couldn't understand that so much time had passed. He looked at me and said, "I canceled it." And he walked away. I was crushed. I felt like a fool. I felt betrayed. I approached my father and asked him why—he made no answer—shrugged his shoulders and walked away. I felt this rejection for a long time. Fifty years later, it returns to me with every bit of its emotional impact.

Recently, I read the following in a biography of Henri Nouwen, a noted Catholic priest and author. This seems to me a logical explanation for my father's behavior.

The father-son relationship is by definition a sensitive one, with its unexpressed competition and its silent battle for precedence.

Passing On

Lunch time activity was not always consistent. Some days were extremely busy and other days were steady, but not overwhelming. This one particular day after an average mid-day rush, I told my father I was going home to join Georgia for lunch. I was there for a short time when a waitress called me to hurry back as my father was not well. I went straight to the café, but the waitress told me that he was next door at the stationery shop. I found him there sitting on a chair and consoling him were Mr. and Mrs. Stimble, proprietors of the shop. As I approached my father, I saw how a part of his face and lip were drooping, his eyes were glazed and tears were crawling down his cheeks. One of his arms hung listless, and the other arm kept hitting his lap repeatedly as if in frustration. He was unable to utter a word. We all felt helpless. I kept pleading with him to tell me what was wrong, how could I help.

I glanced up toward the entrance and to my surprise Dr. Goldberg was passing by. I ran out and told him frantically about my father. He came immediately and exclaimed, "He's had a stroke!" He called for an ambulance, and when the attendants placed him on the stretcher, I noticed that he was still wearing his apron.

I went into the café and told the waitresses the apparent diagnosis and that my father was hospital bound. They told me that he'd appeared his normal self after I left. He had taken some bread crusts, chopped them into little pieces and threw them on the sidewalk for the pigeons, and he came back in and announced that he was going to the stationery shop.

I left the café, picked up my mother and Georgia and went straight to the hospital. Dr. Goldberg gravely told me that my father had a massive stroke and to pray that the Lord take him, for if he were to survive he would be a living vegetable. I knew my vibrant, energetic and determined father could never accept a fate such as that, and by the grace of God, he died peacefully at 11 p.m. that night.

When the funeral arrangements were made, my mother requested that the procession pass in front of the café. As we did so, I remember her saying softly in Greek, "This is the place that consumed your father." She put this so simply yet so truthfully.

The café was closed for three days and then, once again, I placed the key in the door ready to perpetuate what had been established so many years ago. The words of Alfred Lord Tennyson came to mind as I unlocked the door and entered the café for the first time without my father's imposing presence—"The old order changeth to the new."

Finding Bliss

Ben, Jan, and their family arrived in the Soo from Detroit. Ben was a tall, well-built, commanding man with a brusque manner and an air that oozed confidence. He patronized our café quite frequently, alone or with his wife, and occasionally with his whole family.

When Ben visited the restaurant, usually late in the afternoon when there were few other customers, he would often come up to the ledge in our open kitchen and tower over me to chat. Sometimes he would thrust a loaf of bread at me and exclaim that he had gotten it in Greektown in Detroit over the weekend. One day he saw me standing idly and invited me to sit with him. After the usual brief chatter, I asked him how he came into the field of journalism. Ben was a native of Detroit, and after he graduated, he decided to become an engineer. He was in his second year of college when World War II broke out. Shortly thereafter, Ben found himself in Germany where he became involved with the Army newspaper, Stars & Stripes. During his time in the service, he did a lot of reflecting on his interests and experiences. Ben realized that even in engineering school he was always getting involved with theater, theater promotion and publicity, and he enjoyed writing for the school newspaper. His classes were all that he could bear of engineering, but his interests and spare time were always focused in the field of journalism and theater promotion. When the war ended and Ben became a civilian, he gave up on engineering, realizing that it was not his calling. He enjoyed photography, and wherever he went, his camera was always with him. After he married and his family began to grow, Ben decided that Detroit was not the place to raise his children. He had the opportunity for an academic position at our local college, and so he came.

I admired how Ben realized and acknowledged his true interests and honored that about himself. Here was a man who had found his bliss. Joseph Campbell once wrote, "Find your bliss and all else will fall into place." I envied him.

Before the war, my father and some loyal customers convinced me that America was business-oriented and that accounting was to be the heart and soul of the business world. With this advice, the fall after graduating from high school found me enrolled at Cleary College in Ypsilanti, Michigan. This was my first time away from home, living in a rooming house with students attending Cleary and Eastern Michigan University, then called Ypsilanti Normal. I found the courses utterly boring: economics and accounting were, to me, devices designed by the devil. Business English was my only palatable subject. The school newspaper, The Clearyan, needed staff, and I joined. Sometime in mid-winter I became the editor. In the meantime, I continued to find economics and accounting distasteful and overwhelming, and I began playing hooky—something I never would have done in high school.

I discovered that not far from Ypsilanti was Ann Arbor, the home of the University of Michigan, and it was an easy shot to hitchhike there. People in those days were most generous and willing to pick up hitchhikers. I soon discovered the Rackham Building on the campus. At Rackham, free lectures were given on a variety of subjects. Soon I found myself hitchhiking from Ypsilanti to Ann Arbor regularly to attend these lectures. They were a breath of fresh air as opposed to the stale, distasteful accounting and economics courses I endured as part of the business curriculum at Cleary. In the Rackham Lecture Hall, I had found "my bliss", but neglected to acknowledge what was happening to me. Near the end of the school year I was miserable in my business curriculum. I sat down with my small Greek-English dictionary and wrote two or three pages to send my father, explaining to him I was not happy being there. I was wasting time and money. Could I come home? I mailed the letter and waited for his reply hoping to be released from what to me was a nightmare. Several days came and went. One day a postcard came from my father. His answer to my long letter was brief and to the point and quite a reflection on Greek wisdom. He wrote (in Greek), "You ate the cow—now eat the tail!" So I tolerated the last six weeks, until the Greyhound bus took me home.

I never returned to Cleary College, Ypsilanti Normal, or The University of Michigan. My life took another turn. As I sat that day listening to Ben's story of self-discovery, I knew that I, too, had had an opportunity to be in a field that I loved, but I didn't have the strength to go against what my father believed was right and counter his hopes or intentions for me. I chose a path that was laid out for me and carried on my father's work in the restaurant business. Yes, business, my least favorite of subjects.

Acknowledging that all clouds have a silver lining, I must admit that the best part of my life's work as a small-town café owner and cook was the wonderful array of customers and the stories they inspired and shared. In this way, each day was a new discovery, a little "playing hooky" and a mini-lecture in life, occasionally removing me from the mundane business part of my day.

Chris and Sam Gianakura. This is the only picture I have of my father and uncle together. I had this enlarged and framed on display on one of the walls facing the booth customers.

My Uncle Sam in front of the ice cream parlor, just about where the Avery Center sits today on the corner of Ashmun and Maple Streets. In the basement is where he made the candy.

All decked out for Christmas in 1907. My Uncle Sam put in a lot of work preparing for Christmas business. My father, wearing a suit, is on the right. The man on the left in apron is my Uncle Sam. The stack on the left corner is peanut brittle in solid form, usually it is broken in pieces. This location was the same as the previous photo.

My Uncle Sam on the left, customers in the back. The bottles on the left were Root Beer or Sarsparilla, both popular then. We have one light shade that came from this fixture on the left and right. The round boxes on top of the wall fixture hold straws.

Gianakura Brothers to Move to New Location
Will not Occupy Fuoco Block as Formerly Planned

The Gianakura brothers, owners of the American Ice Cream Parlor on Ashmun Street will move into the Soo Theatre building. They will occupy two of the stores, giving them a floor space of 40 by 36 ft.

Their present store is located in the building purchased by the Kresge Co. and their lease expires on April 1, 1930. A month ago the two brothers purchased the Fuoco Block on Ashmun Street south, with the intention of moving their store to that location. Recently they have come to a decision to continue to rent the store space in the Fuoco block to its present occupants, the Soo Oldsmobile Company and move into two of the new theatre stores.

The partition is being taken out between the two stores and it was announced that the Gianakura store will move into its new location April 1.

Copy from the March 11, 1930, article in *The Evening News* regarding the relocation of the restaurant.

The American Ice Cream Parlor on Ashmun Street had hand made candies in the right showcase, my Uncle Sam standing among them. The marble ice cream fountain is on the left. The round marble fixture dispensed plain drinking water and soda water for making ice cream sodas, coca-cola and other soft drinks. Against the right wall holding the mirrors is a beautiful solid oak frame. This was moved to the Soo Theatre location in 1930. I covered it with molded masonite to give the Café a more up-to-date appearance in the 1950's. Fortunately, the Soo Theatre restoration crew saved it when they tore down the facade. Several months later Fran Hoholik spent many months restoring it and the frame is again in its original location.

Above: In the early 1950's. The sign on the air conditioner in the back above the juke box warns high school students not to smoke. The man with coffee to his lips is one of the Greek immigrants I write about. Man in the foreground is Joe "Buck" Baccari, a friendly fellow with many brothers. Next to me is Shirley, the waitress, then my father and Irene Bonnee. Waitresses in those days always wore uniforms, no slacks were permitted. The booths were originally made from solid oak, finished in a silver gray. They were purchased in 1930. One booth is in the Chippewa County Historical Society waiting to be refinished and assembled.

Chris Gianakura and the popcorn stand in front of the American Café next to the Soo Theatre during the 1930's.

Facing page and above: The Café was completely remodeled in the 1960's These pictures were taken from the back. The booths were remodeled by removing the coat hangers and replacing them with chrome ones. The mirrors were removed from the booth walls and the booths were sprayed with a gray lacquer finish covering the original silver gray finish which was beginning to wear. Hiding behind the diamond-patterned facade is the oak frame, since rediscovered and restored. The ever present Coke machine reminds me that when I was very young, I thought my name was Peter Coca-Cola. "Gianakura" was hard to pronounce, and Coca-Cola was everywhere. It made sense to me.

This is a picture of the front of the Café after remodeling in the 1960's. By removing the middle entrance, we gained two booths for increased seating capacity.

Our 70th Anniversary earned us a full-page in *The Evening News* sponsored by the downtown merchants. We hosted an open house and served cake all day. From left to right are Paul Andary, owner of Andary and Sons; Fred Lee, a jeweler at Mackie-Bennett Jewelry Store; Georgia Gianakura; Marvin Dahlman, Mayor and Lake Superior State University professor; Jack Hauck, Manager of Montgomery Ward; and me.

PETE GIANAKURA

Honor Pete On His Anniversary

Downtown Sault merchants and friends of Pete Gianakura, American Cafe proprietor, are sponsoring an open house at the restaurant Saturday morning, celebrating the 70th anniversary of the founding of the business.

The business was opened as an ice cream parlor by Pete's father, Chris Gianakura and Chris' brother Sam, in a West Portage Ave. location near the railroad depot.

Over the years, the business occupied nine different locations, and at one time early in the century, operated from two different locations simultaneous-ly, one on W. Portage Ave., and one o nE. Spruce St., just east of Ashmun St.

In Feb., 1907, the Portage Ave. shop was sold and the business consolidated into one location, the Newton Block on Ashmun St., just south of Spruce St. Renamed the American Ice Cream Parlor, the Gianakura brothers did business in this location for the next 23 years. This location was terminated when the Newton Block was purchased by S.S. Kresge Co. as a site for a new store here.

At this time the business was moved to its present location next to the Soo Theater, into a newly-constructed business block, which it has occupied ever since.

As nearly as can be determined, the American Cafe is the oldest continuously operated restaurant in the city.

The community was invited to celebrate our 70th Anniversary in this article as well as the full-page ad referenced on page 38.

39

AMERICAN CAFE

Dear Friends, Neighbors, Customers:

Your beautiful and unexpected acknowledgment of our 70th anniversary overwhelmed us.

We hope we can continue to merit the kind words and friendship.

It is a testimony to the warm-heartedness of the businesses and people of Sault Ste. Marie and area. Our founders, Chris and Sam, felt this warmth throughout their lives. The busy, steady pace of living, the increased tempo has, somehow, not diminished this warmth.

What a grand way to end a good year and to welcome a new one. Thank you all.

To each and every one of you we wish a happy, healthy and prosperous new year.

Sincerely and gratefully yours,
Peter & Georgia Gianakura
THE AMERICAN CAFE
"Next to Soo Theatre"

Peter & Georgia Gianakura

Georgia and I were so appreciative, we thanked the community with this ad.

Cafe serves Sault since 1902

SAULT, Mich.—"The American Cafe—Serving the Soo since 1902," the motto above the door reads.

The present owner, son and nephew of the founders, seems to have the same feeling for the store that his father and uncle did. Pete Gianakura is preserving the old along with the new.

His father, Chris Gianakura, and his uncle, Sam Gianakura, were new in America and working for the Northwestern Leather Company of the Sault in the early 1900's. They decided their future lay elsewhere, and opened "The American Ice Cream Parlor" across from the railroad depot on Portage St. They bought the dairy goods to make their ice cream from local farmers and sold it mostly to passengers getting on and off the train.

The store has been in nine different locations in its 75 years of existance, most of them centered around the depot.

Sam left town several times over the years, each time bringing back new discoveries. Once he learned to make homemade candies, which the brothers sold in their store. Another time, he brought home the ice cream cone, a new thing to Sault residents. So new was it, in fact, that those eating the treat ate the ice cream and threw the cone away. "They had to teach them that the cones were edible, too," laughs Gianakura.

In time, the brothers added sandwiches and light lunches to their menu. They owned a silent movie theater for a time and were the first eating establishment to convert from gas to electric lights. Their nickelodeon, also the first in the Sault, attracted many people.

The longest time the ice cream parlor was established in one place was in a store at the present location of S.S. Kresge, where they were for almost 25 years.

Since 1934, it has been at its current location, 532½ Ashmun St. Originally, the store took up two buildings. "There was an archway and 12 eating booths next door and long showcases for the candy here," the present owner said. "But then, the Depression came along." The brothers, Chris trying to raise a family and Sam dying of cancer, were short of money and were forced to close half of the store. The archway was cemented in and the other half was rented out separately.

Looking around the present store, it is hard to tell that times have changed. Gianakura points out the tables, which are about 54 years old. He also indicates the eagle which hangs on the wall. "My father had a golden eagle hung in the old store across from the railroad. Under it hung a sign that said, 'I discovered the new world.' Well, I saw an eagle in a catalog, and I sent for it. It's hanging there. It seems right."

But times did change, and homemade ice cream and candy no longer were profitable. Mass-produced items were cheaper. The ice cream parlor became a cafe.

People, too, have changed. "I used to be a soda jerk," says Gianakura. "Whole families would come downtown to windowshop. They'd start down at the Portage end of Ashmun and by the time they got here, they'd be thirsty. Television, or something, has changed all that. You don't see the unity anymore.

"Eating has changed, too," he continued. "It used to be more leisurely at one time."

Some good things have come about from mass production, says Gianakura. For example, it is possible to have a larger variety of food available to the public, and sanitary conditions have improved.

All the same, the American Cafe doesn't seem to have changed very much. Maybe it's a good thing. "We need an anchor on the past," Gianakura says, smoothing the half-century-old tabletop. The American Cafe is just such an anchor.

Ar article from *The Evening News*, April 1979.

41

Backwards signs make lots of mirror sense

HAVE A GOOD DAY

ENGLISH MUFFIN
* TOASTED
* BUTTERED
* WITH JELLY
40¢

FOR GOODNESS SAKE .....COME AGAIN.....

Gianakura's backwards signs make sense

BY W.T.RABE
Special to News

SAULT STE. MARIE + The American Cafe is that Ashmun street restaurant with the signs painted backwards, only nine booths and nine stools at the counter, a full liquor license, but no martinis, which closes most days at 5 p.m.

Detroiters have tried to buy its liquor license, which is valued in the neighborhood of $35,000, but owner Peter Gianakura, who says he doesn't sell a bottle of hard liquor a week, isn't interested.

"I have the license because a few of my customers like a glass of wine with their supper or a bit of brandy with coffee. But I don't have a bar because it wouldn't look right with my family customers."

His menu has such homey observations as "if you are on a vacation and are in a hurry, you are not on a vacation."

You don't notice the backwards signs at first.

Then, you suddenly realize there's something odd about the fact that, in addition to the front of the sign advertising the menu, you can also read, in the mirror, the slogan on the back of the sign.

To set his two-way signs, Gianakura had to persuade a sign painter to work backwards.

"He did okay," he said,"except for the back of the sign in backward Greek. But hardly anyone notices his mistake."

The American Cafe has always been something special in the Sault. Gianakura's father, Christopher, came to town in 1900 from Greece. He planned on opening a pharmacy but his long apprenticeship in Greece didn't mean anything here. He worked around town and then, in 1902, opened a little candy and tobacco shop near the depot. Eight locations later, he settled

down near the Soo Theater, Peter was born in 1922 and within a few years began a career that has him working at 7 a.m., open at 8 and doing most of the cooking from the open kitchen.

The hot beef sandwich, in the early days called "noon lucheons" and selling for 45 cents, is the oldest specialty, now $2.50. But chili, added to the menu only three years ago, is a hot contender.

"Peter makes a great bowl of chili," says Sault native Don Gerrie. "Blasts the roof of your mouth off."

Peter's omelettes are as good as any Frenchman's, according to some locals, and he makes them of any type. If you don't like what's on the menu, bring your own extras, like anchovies.

"There aren't really nine boots," Peter confesses. "I added those two half booths in small corners. They're for people who want private conversations, but they have to be skinny."

The Evening News article about my "backward sign" concept.

42

Gianakuras say farewell to family restaurant business

SAULT STE. MARIE - Peter and Georgia Gianakura have said farewell to the American Cafe in downtown Sault Ste. Marie, turning over the 87-year-old family business to new owners.

"The old order changeth to the new," Gianakura quotes from Alfred, Lord Tennyson, in announcing the sale of the small cafe and long-time businessman's coffee rendezvous at 532 1/2 Ashmun, in the same building as the Soo Theater. New owners are Tanya and Ernest Beaumont who began operation of the cafe this week.

They say they plan to keep both name and menu, but are immediately expanding operational hours which had been cut back in recent years. They will be open until 7 p.m. during the weekend, until 10 p.m. on Friday and Saturdays.

Gianakura says 43 years as owner, manager, cook and genial host of the small cafe have finally reached their natural end. "It was a case of 'burn-out' the last two or three years...It's time for someone else," he said. "The only thing I want to do with food from now on is eat it."

A lifetime in cafe work was not in his plans back in 1946, he said, when he got out of service after five years in the army. He had helped in the family business along with his brothers and sisters summers and weekends all through high school and felt he could rest up from army service and help his father, Chris, for a few weeks. The time stretched to 43 years, working first with his father and then, when the senior Gianakura died of a strike at the age of 88 in 1961, as the owner.

The business itself was started as a family enterprise, by Chris and his younger brother Samuel, who had come from Greece and worked for a while at the local tannery. They soon decided they would prefer another line of work and opened a small store along Portage, across from the then very active railroad depot, selling candy, gum and tobacco to travelers.

Sam went to Chicago to study candy and ice-cream making, and the two brothers began expanding their business, at one time having nine stores.

Although they occupied various locations, the one most older Sault residents will probably remember, Gianakura said, is in the old Kresge building, just down from the corner of Spruce and Ashmun, in the same block where the cafe is now located. When Kresge took over the entire area in the mid-30s, the brothers rented the space of 532 Ashmun for their American Ice Cream Parlor.

After the war and when Sam died, the business changed, dropping the candy and ice cream and becoming a cafe with sandwiches, full meals and snacks.

It faced hard times during the depression years, Gianakura said, and finally his father was able to cut back into just one-half the space, with the other side walled off, to reduce his rent and allow him to stay in business.

Beer, wine and liquor had been added when they became legal, he said, but never were an important part of the business, and more recently he dropped them from the cafe.

Gianakura was always the chief cook, although Georgia worked in the cafe for a time, as did his three daughters. Over the years the menu changed, adding more and more fast foods and cutting back on full meals as the pace of life in downtown Sault Ste. Marie speeded up.

Gianakura recollects the days when the cafe was open in the evenings, to accommodate downtown strollers who would walk to the locks, visit the bandstand, window shop and then "stop by Pete's" for a soda.

More recently he began closing weekends, holidays and eventually after the lunch trade stopped at 3:30 p.m.

Lunchtime business remained brisk, with professional people dropping by as much for a chat as for a sandwich, visiting from one to another of the seven full and three single booths and the seven stools. The exchange of comments and friendly atmosphere led to many lasting friendships developing there, he said.

"We are most fortunate and blessed that two generations of Gianakuras had the opportunity to serve you, the Soo, since 1902," Gianakura said. "Now it's time to go."

A farewell article published in *The Evening News*.

Our "Thank You" to our patrons, also published in *The Evening News*.

43

SLOW ME DOWN LORD

Ease the pounding of my heart by the quieting of my mind.
Steady my hurried pace
With a vision of the eternal reach of time.
Give me, amidst the confusion of my day,
The calmness of the everlasting hills.
Break the tensions of my nerves
With the soothing music of the singing streams
That live in my memory.
Help me to know the magical restoring power of sleep.
Teach me the art of taking minute vacations of slowing down.
To look at a flower;
To chat with an old friend or make a new one;
To pat a stray dog; to watch a spider build a web;
To smile at a child; or to read from a good book.
Remind me each day
That the race is not always to the swift;
That there is more to life than increasing its speed.
Let me look upward into the towering oak
And know that it grew great and strong
Because it grew slowly and well."

ON THIS DAY

Mend a quarrel; search out a forgotten friend; dismiss suspicion, and replace it with trust; write a love letter. Share some treasure. Give a soft answer. Encourage youth. Manifest your loyalty in a word or deed.

Keep a promise. Find the time. Forego a grudge. Forgive an enemy. Listen. Apologize, if you were wrong. Try to understand. Flout envy. Examine your demands on others. Think first of someone else. Appreciate. Be kind, be gentle, Laugh a little more.

Deserve confidence. Take-up arms against malice. Decry complacency. Express your gratitude. Worship your God. Gladden the heart of a child. Take pleasure in the wonder and beauty of the earth. Speak your love. Speak it still again. Speak it still once again.

Compliments of
American Cafe
Serving the Soo since 1902
Next to the Soo Theatre

I was impressed by the thoughts and views on these cards. I wanted to share them with my customers, so I had them printed by the hundreds and made them available near the cash register. They were accepted, and I had pleasant responses from those who read them. Some customers would return and ask for extra copies to share with friends and relatives.

44

A Celebration of Living

A Café of Characters

It would be impossible to write about the customers who patronized our café in a chronological order. Certain circumstances might just bring into focus a time frame. Some of the customers were "regulars" and as time passed, we became acquainted with their extended families. Some of the customers were tourists, some salesmen. They were all unique, and they created situations that are memorable. I might leave some precious moments untold, but, like everything else, I'll just have to take my chances and let the chips of memory fall where they may.

Fathers, Brothers and Sons

One morning a young father came in with his two sons. I had seen the father several times before with his parents, uncles and wife, but this was the first time I had seen him come in with his own young sons, perhaps five and eight years old. They sat in a booth, gave the waitress their order and when she left their table, I saw the two boys whisper in their father's ear. The father pointed to the back of the café, and I heard him tell them to be careful of the stairs. The café's lavatory facilities were in the basement. They shyly and slowly proceeded to the back and down the steps. All was quiet. They were the only customers in the café at the time. A few minutes went by and suddenly we heard screams and loud voices yelling, "Daddy, Daddy!" and quick, scrambling footsteps coming up from the basement.

The boys excitedly ran straight to their father in a state of panic. This was completely different from the disposition they had when they first came in—their shyness suddenly switched to youthful animation. They spoke in loud whispers, arms waving and pointing to the basement. The father listened intently, soothed the boys and spoke to them quietly and confidently. After they ate he came up to me to explain what had disturbed them. The boys had been brought up in the country using outhouses all their short lives. Even the little country school house they attended had outhouses. Here they were in the "big city," their needs for the moment had to be responded to, but they had never used or seen a real, true toilet. The whole thing was an adventure to them and, being curious, they fiddled with the handle of the toilet bowl. When the water was released and the toilet flushed, the sound was strange to their ears, and they panicked.

The father of these two boys had two uncles. They both worked in town at the local plant. They developed a habit of stopping by for a beer or two before going home. They were hard-working farm folk, and I'm sure they probably did a lot of chores early in the morning before driving in to work from the country. When they got home, they were faced with more chores. The shorter and younger of the two, Arthur, appeared to do most of the shopping. He was always coming in with parcels and packages. One time, he came in with two large bags of groceries. He asked if he could leave them with us and he would be back soon to pick them up. The café was small, but we did have some space up front behind the window. The bags were placed there. Eleven p.m. came, time to close up and go home. The grocery bags were still there. Two, then three days went by. We forgot all about them, just as the customer had. Soon a horrible odor surrounded the area. My father opened the grocery bags to find the cause. Raw chickens were rotting. We disposed of them in a hurry. When Arthur finally came for his usual beers, we told him about the bags of groceries he had left and what we finally had to do with them. He looked at us quizzically. He had no idea what we were talking about. He had forgotten entirely.

On another occasion, he came in hurriedly, handed me a fish bowl with gold fish in it and said he would be back to pick it up soon. Soon? A day or two went by and the fish were still on the shelf waiting to be picked up. I decided to run out and get some fish food. They were fed, kept alive until he made his appearance. Again he had forgotten even purchasing them. Although he was a regular, there would be days we wouldn't see him. Shift work around the clock kept him from regular patronage.

One morning he came in with a large, tall package wrapped in brown paper. I asked what he had in it since it was much different than his usual bundles. He told me he had a nephew in the service who was stationed at an Army base. The nephew had written home saying he was very lonesome. So Arthur decided to do something about it. He bought a canary, bird cage and all, and he was going to ship it to his lonesome soldier nephew. In those days, there was no such thing as UPS or Federal Express—the American Railway Express did the job. But, it's a wonder the bird and its cage ever reached its destination.

Arthur asked if I would like to see the bird, and he began to unwrap the package. There was a handsome bird cage and a brightly feathered bird. "I'm sending this to my nephew in the Army. He's lonesome," he repeated and as he spoke, he opened the little door to the cage and instantly the bird flew out. Fortunately, there was just the waitress there besides us. Lord knows what would have happened had we been busy. I suddenly realized my biggest fear was the bird getting caught in the kitchen exhaust fan. After several exciting moments wondering how to capture the little bird, we decided to wrap a towel around a broom and when it got into a corner, cover it with the makeshift trap. We finally caught it in that manner. Arthur was always full of surprises.

The Counter Attack

A busy morning one summer day left us overwhelmed. We had but one waitress. The customers seemed to come in all at once. When the activity ended, and all the customers left, every booth was loaded with empty, dirty dishes, glasses and silverware. The waitress and I cleared off the tables. To save footsteps we piled them up on the counter.

Immediately behind the counter were the sinks for dishes and glasses. There were no customers for a brief spell, until a young man in his 30's came in, sat at a booth just opposite the counter, and ordered coffee. My father was busy preparing food for the impending lunch crowd, and then he came to me where the waitress and I were busy tackling the dirty dishware.

We spoke to each other about some matter, when suddenly the customer in the booth said in a loud voice, "Leave that old man alone." I was surprised by this, but I looked up, offered a smile disbelieving what I heard, and continued to talk to my father. Again the man uttered his strange command. Again I looked up, smiling quizzically, and I continued to talk. Suddenly the man spoke louder, demanding and threatening, but this time he left the booth.

With quick steps he had climbed over the stools, jumped up on the counter, sending dishes and glasses falling and breaking to the floor and into the sink. In a split second he jumped on top of me. We both fell to the floor, he on top of me, my back flat against the floor behind the counter. The waitress screamed as I lay there staring into the man's angry face. His eyes were glaring, and he appeared to be under a spell.

I noticed his mouth was emitting a frothy spit and his arms and hands were flailing across my face as if he wanted to strike me. For some reason he missed hitting me, in spite of his attempts. I look back on this, and I thank God he did not connect. I quickly surmised this man was not in his right senses.

In the meantime, my father was beating the man's back with his fists. The waitress was too dumbfounded to do anything. I yelled to her to call the police. She ran to the phone, only to return to tell me she did not know the number. This was long before 911. Finally I told her to run out in the street and find a policeman, or anyone.

As we tussled, struggled and squirmed, we wound up from behind the counter out in front, on the main floor, next to the juke box. Somehow I managed to switch positions. Now he was on the bottom and I was on top. My concern was to keep him pinned down so that he could not strike. It seemed like an eternity, but finally help arrived. The waitress happened to see our landlord talking to one of the prominent plumbers in town in front of the theatre, next door to the café.

They came running in and the plumber pulled me off, taking my place in holding the man down. The police were called, and my attacker was hauled away to the police station. A quick glance at the damaged inventory showed a few broken glasses, cups and saucers, and my eyeglasses that were bent out of shape.

Late that afternoon the policeman who patrolled the main street at that hour came in and told me that the fellow was arrested and put in a jail cell. Still flushed with anger, he began to hit the jail wall with his fist. He broke his wrist and had to be taken to the hospital. The next day the same policeman came by and gave me some background on this man. It was discovered that, during the winter months, and up until the "counter attack" he had patronized a popular hamburger spot on top of the hill. He was smitten with one of the waitresses there. Day after day he tried to ask her for a date. She was not interested, but he was a persistent fellow. He assumed he was making progress and that she would break down and accept his invitation for a date. The night before his madness, he saw her leave her shift with another man. He was heartbroken and must have brooded all night only to come to the café where his frustrations exploded.

I did not see the man again until I looked out the window one evening. There he was with his date (not the one he was

49

pursuing), standing in line, waiting to get to the cinema next door. Our eyes met quickly, and then he turned his head. A few minutes later he came into the café. With a sheepish grin, and a soft voice, he apologized for attacking me. Since he seemed sincere we shook hands, and he left.

Several months later he began to patronize the café on a regular basis, every Saturday afternoon. We became friends, and bygones became bygones. Much later he retired and moved away. I never did see him again, but he certainly left a lasting impression.

Rick Malone

Rick was a tall, well-built man. He was a construction worker and his employment was subject to the vagaries of the industry. In the late 1940's, employment was an "iffy" affair. Many of our steady customers would usually sit at the counter and, when available, choose the stool closest to the kitchen and coffee urn. When Rick came in, he would head for this stool. He was not much for long conversation. He would utter a reflection of his thoughts on the news of the day and these observations would usually be bitter, sarcastic, condescending and laced with wry humor. One time he pronounced, "Hey Pete—you've heard of swing and sway with Sammy Kaye? Well, moan and groan with Rick Malone."

One day he came in without a jacket. He always wore a jacket but now, jacketless, one could see he was wearing wide suspenders. I had never seen him dressed in this way and suspenders were not that popular. He sat down for his usual cup of coffee, established a poker-faced expression and became lost in thought. Noticing the suspenders, I remarked about them and he nodded his head and a sad expression enveloped his face. "Gotta wear them, Pete. Have a bad back. Can't stand using a belt. Have had lots of trouble and pain." He spoke laconically with pauses between his remarks and assumed his sad, poker-faced look. He sat there for quite some time and every so often he would shake his head and wince as if in pain. When he was ready to leave, he got off the stool, stretched and yawned and came up to me in the kitchen and said, "Pete, just want to tell you I wear suspenders to keep my pants up." And with a loud guffaw, he left.

One morning he came in, sat on his usual stool and I greeted him with, "Big day today, Rick—the dedication of the Mackinac Bridge. The mayors of St. Ignace and Mackinaw City, the Governor and bridge engineers and state officials are going to cut the ribbon in the middle of the bridge. Bands will be playing—big day." He nodded his head, lit his usual cigarette, sipped his coffee and assumed his usual facial expression. He sat in this manner for a long time and after a while his face began to assume a faint smile, the smile became a grin, he took off his hat. This, I recalled, was something he rarely did. He had a healthy head of hair, most unruly, uncombed. His hat was truly a shelter for his head of hair. In removing his hat, he scratched his head vigorously, replaced his hat on his head, and began to laugh. At first a chuckle, barely audible, then his laugh increased and loud guffaws followed as he slapped his thigh—his behavior was as if someone had told him a really funny joke and it tickled his fancy. Out of curiosity I asked him what was so funny. When he finally settled down from his laughing spasms, he said, "Just thinking about all the hoopla at the bridge today with the governor, dignitaries and bands, then at the moment the ribbon is cut, the bridge collapses," and he renewed his laughter. This was Rick Malone.

Rick had a younger brother. He came in one day and asked if he could borrow 50 cents. I gave him the 50 cents and he promised he would pay me within a week. From that day until he was found dead a few years later, he avoided me. If he saw me coming toward him on the sidewalk, he would cross the street. He was a likeable fellow, and I felt sad that a mere 50-cent piece had come between us and damaged a pleasant acquaintance.

The time had come to remodel and freshen up the café. The contractors said it would take a week. It took a month.

We finally re-opened for business. We welcomed our regular customers and greeted new ones. As time went by, I noticed that Rick wasn't coming in, and yet I saw him walking up and down the street. One of his habits was to lean on and drape himself over a parking meter and drink in the activity. One day, I stopped and told him we missed seeing him at the café, and was anything wrong? He looked down and said that our remodeling had made the Café too fancy for him, and he didn't feel right coming in any more. It's strange and sad how circumstances that seem insignificant can so dramatically change relationships.

The Greek Dandies

Several Greek men in the Soo truly stood out as the "Beau Brummels" of their day. With their gray spats over their shiny black patent leather shoes, their three-piece black suits pressed with a sharp, knife-like edge, shirts white and stiffly starched, tie clasps and cuff links shining brightly and, on their heads, they wore either a black homburg or a derby hat. From their vests hung gold watch chains. One sported a well-groomed black moustache that extended beyond the confines of his upper lip and curled and twisted on each end like quotation marks. He was just an ordinary laborer, a tannery employee, but after work he would dress like a professional of the day and unless you knew him you would think of him as a prosperous banker or lawyer. He would come in to the café almost every afternoon and sit at the counter on a stool. There, with great aplomb, he would remove from his suit jacket a gold cigarette case, flick it open, select a cigarette and affix it on a long slender, highly decorated cigarette holder. He would light his cigarette with great flair, his head tilted upward as if he were about to begin a sacred religious ceremony. And perhaps he was, since from that moment on he would stare at his reflection in the large mirrors we had facing the customers. His hypnotic gaze would be broken briefly as he sipped his coffee or took a long, steady drag from his cigarette. To me he seemed to be narcissistically engrossed in himself, or perhaps he was contemplating some major personal dilemma.

Another Greek immigrant dandy wore spats and neatly starched white shirts with conservative ties and pressed suits. On his left little finger, a large diamond solitaire ring shown brilliantly as he flourished his cigarette holder. He was left-handed. In the summer, he wore a straw hat with a black band set at a jaunty angle. He was a cook in a couple of the Greek restaurants in town. He always had a female companion with him, and these women usually conveyed the impression that they were ladies of the night.

On the other end of the spectrum was a man who lived with his brother and his brother's six children. He was a friendly, reserved, and mild man and never associated with anyone on a social basis. He always wore a cap in public. I never saw him without one on his head until I visited the family unexpectedly with my mother and siblings. There he was, minus his head covering, and his hair hung down his back at quite a length. I was stunned since I had never seen a man with such long hair. When I mentioned this to my father, he told me that George should be a monk in a monastery and that he had not truly adapted to the American scene. He was kind and gentle and a loner, having nothing to do with the Greek community, let alone the American citizenry. His main occupation of time was working at the tannery and reading his Bible.

Then there were two others with the same name, George. One worked at the tannery, a quiet loner who dressed in plain, unassuming clothes worn by the typical factory worker of the Depression years. The other was a cook. He dressed neatly and had a most pleasing personality. He was outgoing and always wore a smile. This fellow had been married at one time, and periodically a young lad, who was blond and fair, accompanied him. The young lad was referred to as the cook's son, but I never did see his wife. I assumed they shared custody. One Easter midnight service, the cook made his presence known. The church was small and the incense was thick, both in vapor and aroma. At midnight and all candles and lights were put out. And as tradition has it, the Royal Doors of the iconostasis* were drawn aside and out came the priest with the one and only source of light in the candle he was holding. As he did this, he chanted in Greek, "Christ has risen!" and the congregation responded in unison, "He is truly risen." At that very moment, loud, snapping noises overwhelmed the aura of the service along with sparks and smoke—someone had lit a series of firecrackers near the entrance to the church. The priest, as everyone else, was shocked and stunned and when he gathered his wits, he bellowed, "Who did that? What is the meaning of this intrusion?" It was the Greek cook. He raised his hand and admitted his deed explaining it was a custom in his Greek village—he meant no harm as it was just a means of accentuating the resurrection of the Lord. And as he spoke, he did the sign of the cross fervently and repeatedly. The priest glared at him and reminded him he was not in that village at this time, nor was this behavior appropriate. Then, total silence for a minute, and the reverent decorum of this important service resumed. I was an altar boy that Easter Eve, and I'm glad I was there to witness the thunderous acknowledgement of our Lord's resurrection.

*An iconostasis is a wall of icons in an Orthodox church that separates the sacred altar from the congregation.

Old Man Brown

If Socrates were to appear before us, as I visualize him, I would not be surprised if Γερο George Brown looked exactly like him, but without the beard. Γερο, (pronounced "Yeddo") in Greek, means "old man." In Greek, this term has an air of dignity and respect as opposed to the derogatory feeling one gets when hearing it in English, "Old Man." The name "Brown" is unlike any Greek name.

It is a fact that when immigrants entered the United States

and were asked for their name, if the immigration official had difficulty in pronouncing the name, he would interpret as best he could. George Brown's Greek name was George Vramopoulos. One can respect the turnaround, or the adaptation of the first syllable, "Vram," to Brown, and forget, or overlook, the "opoulos."

How this man came to the Soo, or when, is anybody's guess. Γερο Brown was short and stocky, with a large round head and hardly a neck to separate his head from his strong, broad shoulders. He had a dark olive complexion and small, twinkling eyes.

Brown owned a small store on Portage Avenue, in the heart of the tourist area, near the Soo Locks. He called his store The California Fruit Market. In the early spring through late fall fruits and vegetables and all kinds of tourist-oriented merchandise were on display on the sidewalk in front of his store. In a sense it was a true variety shop.

In time Γερο Brown also put in a popcorn stand. He and my father developed a friendship. In spite of their friendly acquaintance, they never addressed each other by just their first names in all the many years of the relationship; they always addressed each other formally, with title and first name—Mr. George or Mr. Chris.

Γερο Brown worked seven days a week, from morning until he closed his shop at 10 p.m. He would then walk to The American Café, sit in the back booth, order coffee and wait patiently for my father to join him. Here they would sit and discuss world and church affairs in a serious manner. I seldom ever saw them laugh or jest. All conversation was sober. Every so often I would see Γερο Brown's head weaving to and fro, and barely hear him chanting some part of the Holy Liturgy. This he did while waiting for my father to join him in their conversations.

Many times he would expound on the Greek contribution to the world. He would get carried away as his posture straightened, his eyes sparkled, and his voice would rise with enthusiasm. His hands gestured in such a way to emphasize his point. "And, of course," he would declare, "Christopher Columbus was Greek. Who else but a Greek could discover America?"

Close to my high school graduation in 1940, Γερο Brown would attempt to give me fatherly advice on a career. It was always in the world of business. In his broken English he would say with utter conviction, "Business is everything." This I heard dozens of times. I often wonder if this isn't one of the reasons my father persuaded me to attend Cleary College, a small business college in Ypsilanti, Michigan.

Γερο Brown's appearance as a customer at the café was always at night. One summer day, while I was tending the popcorn stand, he walked by, dressed in suit and tie and straw hat. Lo! A small dog was leading him at one end of a leash. I had never seen him walking like this, and with a dog, no less. I greeted him, and asked him what kind of a dog he had? With a huge grin and a twinkle in his eyes he said, in Greek, Ζωον Τετραποδον. With this pronouncement, he walked on with his companion. I did not quite comprehend his remark entirely, so I ran into the café and told my father what I saw, and heard. My father translated, "This, my boy, means 'a four-legged animal.'" So much for the breed.

Their friendship extended to annual invitations to our home on Christmas and Easter. Γερο Brown's Christmas gift to each of us children was always an envelope of money.

Γερο Brown passed away at close to 80 years old. He is buried in our local cemetery. His stone is small, square, and can hardly be called a memorial. It lies flat on the ground. It is difficult to locate. The inscription is plain and simple, with his name, date of birth, and death—too small a remembrance for such a large personage.

Ivan

"Get knowledge, get wisdom, but with all thy gettings, get understanding."

— Anonymous

Ivan was a deaf mute. He was born to a quiet, humble and hard-working immigrant couple from Macedonia. They were devout Christians. They had a daughter and two sons— Ivan was the third and last child. After his father died, Ivan's widowed mother, dressed in black for mourning, attended St. George Greek Orthodox Church every Sunday. I recall sitting behind her and watching her dab her eyes with her hankie throughout the Divine Liturgy, Sunday after Sunday. I was impressed. Now here is a true devout Christian. How seriously she took her faith. How moved she became during the service. This was remarkable, I concluded. Many Sundays passed and I happened to mention my observation to my father who told me that she had an eye affliction that created an uncontrollable flow of tears. Hearing this shattered my impression. Nevertheless the lady was always there at church, dressed in black— humble, sweet and soft-spoken.

In his teens Ivan was hired as a dishwasher in various Greek restaurants in the city. When the government created the Social Security Disability Act he was, blessedly, a recipient of this benefit. When the State of Michigan inaugurated the bottle and can deposit of ten cents for each item, Ivan's pockets bulged with empty cans and bottles which he would later take to exchange for money. Almost every morning I would inevitably see Ivan waiting for me in the café doorway as I started my day. On entering the café, soon after I turned on the lights, he would slowly go from booth to booth, survey the counter and help me prepare for the day by making sure that there were ashtrays and matches at each place. If he ran short he would make guttural noises to get my attention so that I would supply him with products to replace the missing items.

On one of our regular mornings, I unlocked the door and let Ivan in ahead of me. I noticed instead of a can or bottle stuffed in his back pocket Ivan had a magazine rolled up, sticking out quite obviously. I tapped him on the shoulder to get his attention. Whenever I did this it would startle him; he would shrug his shoulders and turn his head quickly. This time, I pointed to Ivan's back pocket and shrugged my shoulders questioningly. He put his head down as if in shame and avoidance, reached back, and gave me the magazine. It was *Playboy*.

Ivan's favorite seat at the café was a small booth against the wall, under the clock, with a view of the street. Although one could not see the Greek Orthodox Church from there, it was only a block away. The priest would periodically make missionary visits to Sudbury, Wawa, and North Bay, Ontario, Canada. There were enough Orthodox people in these areas that it warranted the visit of a priest. The priest in the Soo was the closest, and he was willing to travel to reach the remote locations although it meant abandoning his regular parishioners in the Soo on such occasions. The priest had been a missionary in the Congo for some 30 years, so this missionary duty was part of his training. Ivan, a devoted churchgoer like his mother, would go to church on the Sundays that the priest was traveling and find it locked. Unfortunately, he had no way of knowing the Sundays our priest would be gone and no one thought to let him know. Eventually, Ivan learned to come to the café on Saturday mornings and sit in his favorite booth. He would get my attention, point in the direction of the church, bow his head reverently and hold his hands as if in prayer, look up at me quizzically and wait for my confirmation of whether there were to be services the next day. I would shake my head negatively, forming a silent "no" with my mouth, or positively, as the case might be. If there were to be services Ivan would look at me again, open his mouth, and with a gesture of his hand ask if there were to be refreshments after the service. Not knowing how to read or write, it was admirable how Ivan was still able to convey his wants and needs with mere facial expressions and hand gestures. Necessity is truly the mother of invention.

As the years went by, Ivan acquired a limp. This limp jeopardized his balance and caused his demise. Much time passed, and Georgia and I saw no Ivan. We learned that he had slipped and fallen one late winter day on some ice, and he was hospitalized. We went to see him. He was totally uncommunicative; whereas there had been a time when recognition easily took place—a smile, a hand gesture would say much. We also learned he had lost his eyesight. There was this poor soul—no hearing, no eyesight, crippled, no family—how devastating. This hit us deeply. We felt so helpless. Then, being wrapped up with the café and the myriad of other activities, Ivan slipped to the back of our minds.

As I write this I feel truly saddened. Ivan's circumstances evoke a heavy and profound feeling in me, and I find myself in tears remembering him. I know Ivan rests in peace; most assuredly, he is in the arms of God, whole and talking with his loved ones.

Salvation Army

One busy day I received a call from the captain of the Salvation Army. He asked if I would be willing to serve a meal to anyone they sent to the café with a written request and keep a record of the food consumed to be reimbursed by the Salvation Army? Of course, I agreed. The man assured me they would be discreet and send me individuals who were truly in need. The arrangement worked well. The clients were not overwhelming in number. Many weeks would pass before I would be approached by a person, couple, or small family. Needless to say, I met a great variety of people of various circumstances. The majority of them were quiet and reserved, possibly embarrassed for the position in which they found themselves. They were in dire need and had no choice but to request help. For a very long time this went along quite well and I sent the first few bills that had accumulated and was reimbursed. As time passed

I realized that the cost to the café was not a financial drain. On the contrary, I found it to be a small contribution to mankind in need.

So I began filing the signed and dated guest checks. I never bothered to send them in for reimbursement. Today all these people who once found themselves in need pass through my memory occasionally but one especially stands out.

He was a young man who came in with the usual permit. He had a small suitcase with him and he sat at the counter. It was Friday evening and we were very busy. As I prepared his meal, I saw him light one cigarette after another. This disturbed me. If he could afford to buy cigarettes, I thought, surely he could manage to pay for his food? Throughout his stay he patronized the juke box several times, putting in quarter after quarter. This too alarmed me. The next day I called the Salvation Army about this young man's conduct. They assured me they did the best they could to screen the beneficiaries and they could make mistakes. This was understandable, and I realized one individual taking advantage of the system should not spoil the whole program. And it didn't.

As someone once said, "'Tis better to light a candle than to curse the darkness."

The Phone Call

For many years prior to remodeling, the phone was in the kitchen just a few feet from the refrigerator and the coffee urn. It sat at the end of the sandwich board, handy for me, the employees and the customer who may have need of it. The area was congested and to have an extra person using the phone became a frustrating experience at times. Nevertheless, our customers were free to use it.

Friday nights were always active since the retail stores up and down Ashmun Street stayed open until 9 p.m. Just about 6 p.m., a young lad would appear and ask for the use of the phone. This went on from Friday to Friday. I never saw him in between. He would call his home and always ask for his mother. He came from a large family. One day, I noticed in the obituary column that his mother had died unexpectedly. Friday came and just like clockwork he came in at his usual time, asked to use the phone, told the operator his home phone number (there were no dial phones in those days) and in hearing one of his siblings he asked to speak to his mother. I was quite taken aback with his request, and I quickly looked in his direction. His facial expression was one I will never forget. From an eager, anticipating wide-eyed look, his face became a mask of sadness. His eyes closed, tears ran down his cheeks, his lips quivered as he slowly put the receiver down and walked out of the café. Some time later I spoke to one of his sisters who coincidentally was the one to answer the phone that Friday evening. She explained that her brother had been so in the habit of calling and talking to his mother every Friday that his eagerness apparently overlooked his mother's demise—his loss.

Mother and Son

Beth and her two female companions patronized the café at least once a week. From what I gathered in talking to them they would come to town to shop, meet at the café mid-afternoon and depending on the weather, have a beer or two with a hamburger or coffee and a sandwich. Bits and pieces of conversation I overheard in passing their booth was always about what they had purchased, the bargains they found or juicy bits of gossip. A raised voice would utter some remark such as, "You don't say?!" or "I can't believe what I'm hearing!" or "Oh! And what did she say to that?" As they talked, drank and ate, they puffed on their cigarettes as if they were a part of their sustenance, and they were.

About the only time Beth would come in by herself was on Friday nights. One could set a watch by her arrival. She would appear at 6 p.m. every Friday, sit in the back booth, light a cigarette and order her chicken dinner, the same dinner every Friday for supper. It became such a routine that if I saw her entering the café I would immediately start her chicken dinner. Every so often her son Jerry would come in, always in a hurry, sit down for a brief moment, exchange a few words and leave as quickly as he entered. Beth always wore a smile and her eyes had a constant half-shut appearance as if she were squinting, as if she were either on the verge of falling asleep or had poor vision. She was always full of bits of gossip and because the back booth was so close to our open kitchen, she would burst out with the latest bit of news. Did I know that so and so had a baby? "And Pete," she would utter, "She ain't even married," or "I hear Joe is very sick and may not live to see the weekend."

She loved to pick strawberries when the season rolled around. She would tell me the best time to go. "Have you been to Carley's Strawberry Farm yet, Pete?" she would ask. I knew then that it was time to go and pick them. She loved to attend funerals and many times she would ask me if I attended "so and so's" funeral. Being confined to the café I was not able to attend many funerals. On telling her I had not gone, she would give me the details—if there were many people or not, the color of the deceased's clothing, the number of floral arrangements. At times she would remark, "He always wore glasses, Pete, but he wasn't wearing them this time. I hardly recognized him," or "She never had a permanent in all the years I'd known her. But there she was, fancy permanent and wearing a dress I ain't ever seen on her before. Imagine that!" Or "They sure made a mistake when they fixed his hair. He never parted his hair on the right side!" This was a great part of the Friday news I would hear as Beth waited for her chicken dinner. One day she asked me if I had attended some man's funeral. She felt bad because she was too sick to attend, and she asked me, "How did he look, Pete?" "Dead," I said, and the subject of funerals never came up again.

As the years passed I noticed she began to limp badly and relied on a cane. Then her visits to the café became less frequent. On one of her rare appearances she told me she wasn't able to move around much and couldn't get out like she used to. Her knees and back hurt too much. Every so often I would see her son Jerry, and he would tell me, "Mom's not too good anymore. Can't move too good." He would scurry off in a rapid gait.

A neighbor and his wife took a liking to Beth and her son Jerry. They were always on the lookout for their welfare in many ways. One day I saw their neighbor and asked him how Beth was since I had not seen her in many months. He informed me she had to be admitted to Tendercare, a facility for the elderly who could no longer live on their own. She needed 24-hour care and her son Jerry was not capable of giving it. The friendly and caring neighbors found it overwhelming. Sometime later my mother was admitted to this place, and whenever we visited her we would see Beth in her wheelchair near the door to her room or in the hallway. She was always a "people person" and she was always in the midst of the hustle and bustle of other residents and employees. She would greet us with her squinting eyes and smile and ask how we were doing. My mother was there for nearly a year, but Beth was there for over twelve years.

One sad day we read in the obituaries that Beth had passed away and that she had requested no visitation, no graveside rites—just a burial. That was final. I was not aware of her religious affiliation nor knew much about her background. I had assumed she was a native of the Soo. I called her neighbor, not knowing who else to call, and expressed our sympathy. I told him I was surprised with her passing away without the usual, customary rites. He told me it was her request, since no one came to visit her in all the years she was confined in Tendercare, there was no reason why anyone would come to her funeral. She told her neighbor that when she died she just wanted to be buried—no fuss, no prayers, nothing. And how was Jerry? Not too well, the neighbor said. About the only people to visit Beth regularly were her son Jerry and her neighbor. We commented on the sadness of it all. A few months later the neighbor told me that he had his hands full caring for Jerry because Jerry could not read. "Jerry couldn't read?" I exclaimed. "That's right, and someday I'll tell you about it," he said. When his mother entered the facility for the elderly, he had moved to a high-rise complex that catered to low income seniors. The good hearted, caring neighbor would take him to buy groceries, to the doctor's office and since he could not read, the neighbor would read his prescription instructions to him. A few months later, after his mother passed away, Jerry himself was admitted to Tendercare, just as his mother had been years before. By the time the year ended, Jerry passed away also. His obituary read the same as his mothers. This time there were no survivors.

One day not too long after Jerry's death, I ran into the neighbor once again. I relayed the sadness we felt over this mother and son situation. I guess you don't know the whole story he said, and told me that Beth and Jerry moved to the Soo when Jerry was a mere infant. His father had abandoned them. Beth made a living by cleaning houses, eventually becoming a steady housekeeper for the large local hotel and remained there until she retired. Jerry was her whole life. She was fearful of losing him and afraid of sending him to school. Somehow she managed to keep Jerry's existence a secret until his late teens. Consequently, he never learned to read. Beth was always a friendly, warm person, but her circle of friends was small. It is ironic that she was always curious about the funerals she attended, and yet her passing and Jerry's came and went without a trace that they even existed.

Pain, not Pleasure

A lady began patronizing our café on a steady basis. As she did so we became aware of her timely routine. She would come late mornings and late afternoons five days a week. A cup of coffee and a cigarette were her means of comfort as she sat on one of the stools as close to the kitchen as she could get. She was friendly and became quite open in her conversations with all of us.

We learned that her husband, because of his work, was

always on the road. This left her to raise her four teenagers by herself. We wondered how she could spend so much time in the café with four children and all the demands that face a housewife and mother.

Over time we noticed a change in her personality. When she first began her visits she was quite talkative and easy to communicate with as she sat sipping and smoking. There was constant banter between us. As the days and weeks passed, she became withdrawn. Her bubbling personality diminished and she began to talk to herself in a quiet manner, shaking her head as she prattled inaudibly. Her visits remained constant and timely.

One day, after sipping much coffee (in those days there were endless cups of coffee), and puffing several cigarettes, she burst out in a tirade of swearing, loud and clear. This took us all by surprise. It was such a switch in conduct from previous days.

I approached her and gently asked her if we could help her in some way. Her response was unexpected and quite shocking. "It's those damn kids of mine," she loudly announced. "They give me pain where I should have pleasure!"

The Diet?

Just when I thought I had a fairly good handle on a customer's tastes and I could anticipate their needs, some quirk would pop up and my theory would dissolve. One such case was a teacher who would come in the late afternoon two to three times a week and order the same food item—a special hamburger combination created by my father-in-law when he had his own restaurant. It featured a beef patty with a strip of grilled bacon on top of it. Served open-faced on a bun, the other side was topped with lettuce and tomato. On top of the tomato was placed a decorative swirl of mayonnaise, with a sprinkle of parsley flakes. All in all it made a colorful presentation. We called it a Bacon Burger and nicknamed it a "Bridget Bardot."

When I got to know a customer well enough, I would put his or her initials on the tomato with the mayonnaise, or, if his first name were short, such as "Joe" or "Jim", I would write the name on it. The teacher, short in stature and quite stocky, favored the "Bridget Bardot" which she ordered quite consistently for many months. She would always ask for extra mayonnaise. One day she told the waitress to leave the mayonnaise off completely. "No more mayonnaise," she said. She declared that she was on a diet, but she ordered her customary large Coke as well. After eating her sandwich without mayonnaise, she called the waitress over and ordered a hot fudge sundae. As the waitress went to make it, she called out, "and don't forget the whipped cream and maraschino cherry!"

Lady in Blue

The Dial-A-Ride bus brought several customers to our door, mostly senior citizens. Many of them would enter the café with a cheery greeting, a smile, and a readiness to chat with the waitress, their companions, or me.

There was one short little elderly lady who regularly came to the café accompanied by a young woman who appeared to be her caretaker. Her favorite lunch was a cheeseburger with sweet relish. This was followed by a chocolate sundae. She seemed to be lost in thought and always had a worried, sour expression on her face.

It was her habit to sit in a booth in the center of the café. One time however, she and her companion sat in the back booth. To get to the basement I had to pass by her booth. I stopped and asked her how she was. With a morose look and downcast eyes she said softly, "Not too well. I'm not well at all." I told her I was sorry to hear this.

In spite of her sad outlook she had a motherly, peaceful air about her. I noticed she was wearing a soft blue sweater and around her neck hung a gold chain with a small mother-of-pearl cross—a very lady-like appearance. As we spoke her head was bent down. To continue our brief talk, I remarked that if she had a tummy ache a glass of 7-Up might help. She shook her head slowly. Or, I said, a couple of aspirins. She shook her head again. Then I suggested Anacin. Suddenly her head jerked up, and with a loud, explosive voice she exclaimed, "Those god-damned things don't work either!"

Gert

I imagine just about every town has "bag ladies". The Soo had two of whom I was aware. They could be seen roaming the streets at all hours. Occasionally I would see them walking together, but most times they would be alone. The one I came to know was Gert. That's the name she gave one of our wait-resses. Gert would sit in the front booth, place one full bag on the floor and the other bag on the seat next to her.

Gert was a tall, gaunt lady. She was toothless and this emphasized her large, protruding chin, which was her domi-nant feature. Many cold, bitter nights I would see her pass by the café, walking slowly, bent over with a heavy bag in each hand. I often wondered if she had a place to stay at night. She appeared to be dressed warmly with heavy coat, gloves, and scarves around her neck and usually one that she wrapped around her head.

One day our waitress noticed there was some movement in the bag next to Gert. The waitress asked what that might be and without a word, Gert placed her hand in the bag and pulled out one of the smallest, scrawniest little dogs we had ever seen. It resembled a Chihuahua. Large bulging eyes popped out of his head and he had long curled nails which appeared to have never been trimmed. He had likely never walked about. He was always tucked in the bag. Gert would order coffee and toast, and once in a while she would cut a small piece of toast and feed the little animal while it was still in the bag.

A while later we noticed that she no longer had her four-legged companion with her. The waitress asked about her pet. She was quiet for a while as if she were gathering her thoughts and then she explained, "Well, he's at the Harvard Medical School! When he died, they asked for his body so they could study his brain. He was a genius, you know."

Clyde

You could just about set your watch by the arrival of Clyde. He was a farmer, but farming was a risky occupation being at the mercy of Mother Nature, so he augmented his income by working at the local Union Carbide plant.

Right after work at the plant, Clyde would enter the café. As he headed for the basement, where the lavatories were located, he would slap the counter and shout, "Hey, Pete, give me a goddamn beer right here." It did not bother him if there were any customers, children or women within ear shot. He threw out his oral command to be sure he was heard by all. On his return from the basement he would perch himself on a stool, light a cigarette, and sip his beer in silence. On some occasions he would expound on a variety of subjects, but all on the local level—the weather, hunting, fishing, and the disposition of his farm equipment. A few weeks before Christmas our small café was a madhouse of activity from opening to closing. I hardly had time to think or visit the facility in the basement. On one of those chaotic days he called me from the kitchen. I could scarcely spare a minute, since the kitchen routine demanded a rhythm to keep up with orders. I quickly approached him, and as I did, he moved a $20 bill in front of me. "Here's twenty bucks. Go get a Christmas gift for Bessie." Bessie was his wife. I was stunned and explained to him that I had no spare time. "Impossible," I said. He continued to plead. I assured him I just had no time. Besides, I would have no idea what to get for her. I suggested he ask his three sons to do this. "Hell," he said. "They don't have any more of an idea than I do."Whether Bessie ever received a gift from Clyde that year I never knew, but Christmas came and went, and Clyde continued to slap the counter, shout out his order, and head for the basement.

Duncan Logan

Duncan Logan was a man I could not call by his first name. To me he was always Mr. Logan. He was employed at the local Union Carbide plant located on Portage Avenue just beyond the hydro-electric plant. Mr. Logan and his wife lived in the downtown area and often after a day's work he would stop by the café for an ale or two. Mr. Logan never drank beer; ale was his favorite beverage. The brand of ale that quenched his thirst was Carling's Red Cap Ale, and this was bottled in a distinct green glass; not the typical brown of a beer bottle. One could set his watch by Mr. Logan's appearance. After downing an ale or two, he would head home to his apartment and supper. About 7 p.m. he would return. Instead of his usual work clothes which were a plaid shirt, dark heavy trousers and work shoes, Mr. Logan would appear dressed in a black suit, white shirt and black bow tie. His attire was so formal that one would think he was a funeral director (the dress of the day for that occupation) or perhaps on his way to a wedding or some other such occasion. It was apparent that Mr. Logan must have had a few more ales before returning to us the second time by the way he approached his favorite stool—at the end of the counter near the kitchen—and the way he pulled out his favorite cigarettes, Herbert Tareyton King Size which were long and sophisticated looking with a cork tip. As we knew what he wanted by the gesture of his head, a nod toward the beer cooler, Mr. Logan would soon have his green bottle in front of him.

One day the delivery of Red Cap Ale came to us in brown bottles. I thought it strange and told the delivery man as much.

He told me that was the way it came from the brewery but explained that this was only a temporary condition as they had run out of green bottles. So this particular evening, in came Mr. Logan. I was not fully aware of his fetish for the green bottle. I assumed his love for Red Cap Ale was sufficient. On being presented with his ale in the brown bottle, his reaction was immediate and angry "What's this?" he shouted in an accusatory tone.

I explained that was the way it came from the brewery. "The hell it did—you switched labels!" I was stunned. I went to the cooler, pulled out several brown bottled Red Cap Ales and showed them to him. "Mr. Logan, would I go through all the trouble to do such a thing?" He replied angrily, "Maybe you didn't but the brewery did, I don't want it." And with this, he stomped out of the store.

Red Cap Ale in the green bottle soon came back into circulation and so did Mr. Logan. What he did in the meantime, deprived of his favorite beverage in its trademark container, Lord only knows.

One evening Mr. Logan came in with all the appearance of having a few Red Caps too many. He sat in his usual place, made his customary gesture and soon was quenching his thirst which, apparently, was insatiable. A few minutes after his second bottle and puffing on his Tareyton, he began to recite what I recognized as poetry. Mr. Logan had never done this before in my memory, so I listened attentively. I recognized some well-known lines of Robbie Burns, and there was Mr. Logan reciting this famous Scot's poems in such a manner it would make any true Scot proud. He did not falter, did not hesitate; it all rolled out poetically and beautifully. After a while he stopped, picked up his cigarettes and lighter and stiffly walked out. The next day his wife came in for her afternoon tea. I mentioned to her how impressed I was with her husband's recitation. "Oh", she said, "He must have been in his cups."

"Well," I responded, "I'm going to ask him to do it again." She said that he could not and would not do so unless he had several ales in him. I did not quite believe her so that late afternoon when Mr. Logan came in for his usual ale or two after work, I asked him if he would recite a bit of Burns since I enjoyed his recitation very much the night before. He gave me a quizzical, puzzled look and said, "I don't know what you are talking about."

The Back Booth

Obviously, booths in restaurants play a role in human essentials— basically eating and drinking. On closer observation they are also havens, offering private or semi-private niches that are often so necessary in our daily lives. The back booth at The American Café was no exception.

Early back booth recollections involve the Greek language lessons that I was required to take. Greek letters had to be memorized, Greek words and sentences copied repeatedly—endlessly it seemed—until the Greek letters were created clearly and discernibly. Oh, how boring all this was, especially knowing my classmates and children in the neighborhood were otherwise having fun. My Greek language lessons were expanded on, explained further and drilled aloud by my father in the café's back booth. It became a mini-classroom. And this was true in ensuing years as I found myself involved in the café during junior and senior high school. Much of my homework was done there in the back booth. Still later when our daughters reached the homework stage of their school years, the back booth continued to be used for this purpose.

The back booth was likewise a special space where my father's immigrant friends would discuss Greek politics, church activities and family problems. It was also a secluded spot for high school children who lit their cigarettes and imitated adults in a pseudo-sophisticated way.

Many coffee breaks took place in the back booth and one could hear whispers of excitement and laughter as its occupants planned and talked about their hunting and fishing adventures. Reflecting on my own limited experience with these outdoor activities, I often thought that the planning and anticipation was just about as exciting as the actual events.

Coffee and lunch breaks in the back booth were often business liaisons. I can only imagine how many success stories would develop from these conversations, not to mention failures and disappointments. I could sense the talk of persuasion—sales talk, and although I never did hear the outcome I often wondered how successful the pitch had been: did it bear fruit?

The back booth was the site of many trysts, some socially legitimate and acceptable in nature and others between a man and a woman meeting clandestinely. Over a period of time, one would learn about a divorce among one or both of the parties or find out that the couples involved would break up their affair and each would go their own way—whatever destiny had in store.

In some instances the meetings taking place in the back booth were between a young couple, a young man courting his companion—a Coke before a movie, an ice cream sundae after a movie, a coffee and a roll, a breakfast or a lunch—meetings that took on a predictable regularity. My father could sense this and in a mischievous but sincere and light-hearted manner, he would joke with them, asking them when they were going to marry. Sometimes he would beckon to the young man with a wave of his hand and whisper, "Don't let the young lady get away, marry her, she's a good girl, don't lose her." Inevitably the meetings would culminate in marital bonds—he was a matchmaker. Although I witnessed much of this, I was not interested in playing Cupid. My father was just the opposite. He had a manner that allowed him to get away with such advice and not offend the parties involved. These unions sometimes culminated in the creation of children who, over the years, also became steady patrons of the café.

On many Friday evenings, Georgia and our daughters would have their supper in the back booth. Georgia had a passion for French fries, and although she would never order them for herself, she would manage to pick a French fry or four from each of our daughters' plates in the sanctity of the back booth.

If the booths could talk and relate their observations, record conversations, they surely would claim that they witnessed the entire gamut of the human condition—a complete spectrum of man's conduct would be revealed.

The back booth is now in daughter Joy's possession. She has refinished it to its original condition. Another one of the booths is in the Chippewa County Historical Society museum. It is nice to know the booths have left their mark in spite of their silence.

A Special Couple

As in any business catering to the public, faces come and go. Some may be seen once and never seen again. After an initial visit some come infrequently but are still recognized, and a common bond develops. Other faces come frequently and steadily and depending on their personalities, a friendly acquaintance emerges.

Ben was one such fellow. His favorite time of arrival was usually between 2 and 4 p.m. He would find an empty booth, drop his armful of mail, order coffee, sometimes a hamburger and fries, and in a quick but thorough manner process his stack of mail. For "dessert" he would tackle the Detroit newspaper and out would come his red-inked ballpoint pen which Ben used to complete the crossword puzzle. I was always amazed at how quickly and thoroughly he would fully complete that crossword puzzle, neat and tidy with hardly any hesitation.

One day Ben came in with his usual collection of mail. There was only one booth available and that had just been vacated by a mother and her little daughter. The table still had the dishes and glasses on it, plus a plate of half-eaten French fries. The waitress approached the table to clear it off. As she did, Ben told her to take everything, but leave the French fries. He wanted to eat them, and he munched away as he filtered through his mail.

My wife, Georgia, created a reputation with her bran-apple muffins and Dutch apple pies. Ben took quite a liking to the muffins. One early afternoon he went to the phone and motioned me to come over. As Ben was dialing he told me he was calling a friend of his in Detroit, an announcer named Mike Whorf on the "Great Voice of the Great Lakes," Detroit's famous WJR radio station. Would I talk to him about the muffins? Before I could respond, Ben was talking to Mr. Whorf and he promptly gave me the phone. Ben said, "You are on the air!" I was dumbfounded, but Mr. Whorf came on in such a warm and friendly manner I felt immediately at ease. We discussed the muffins, pie and small-town restaurants. It was near Easter, and Mr. Whorf asked me about the Greek tradition of eating lamb on Easter Sunday. This conversation took place in less than five minutes. Ben was notorious for doing things on the spur of the moment. Not too long after the radio broadcast we had tourists come in and ask about the muffins. They had heard about them when my interview was broadcast on the radio in Detroit. Talk about great publicity!

Ben's wife Jan was a tall, stately woman who was quiet in manner and soft in speech. She and her lady friends would come in quite often in the late afternoons. They would sit in a booth, order their tea and muffins and have a delightful conversation as they talked and laughed—so pleasant and agreeable. They always seemed to have a great time.

One afternoon as the ladies sat and sipped their tea, Ben came in with his usual bundle of mail. As he passed their table he acknowledged their presence by just nodding his head. He went to the next table, deposited his mail, and left the café. He returned moments later with a single rose in his hand purchased down the street at Co-ed Flowers & Gifts, laid it in front of his wife, gave her a quick and gentle kiss, and returned to his table and his mail. Not a word was spoken, but his rose and his gentle gesture spoke preciously.

He was tall, strongly-built and not given to that "hail-fellow well-met" back-slapping pseudo-camaraderie that some easily fall prey to. He was down to earth and yet spontaneous in whatever moved him in a civilized, gentlemanly manner.

A time came when I could no longer work at the café with any zest. I felt burned out and bitter resentment at anything related to the café, and I decided that it was time to sell it. Word of my decision quickly spread around town. When Jan and her lady friends heard about it they were adamant that I should not sell and complained that things would never be the same. What were they going to do and where were they going to go? Every time the group of ladies came in they would ask me if anything had developed and lament on how they hoped the sale of the café would not materialize.

Much time went by with no prospects for a buyer. One day, as the ladies were ready to leave after their afternoon tea, they asked how things were going in my attempts at selling the café. I told them that I had given up, that it was now in God's hands. In response to this comment Jan looked at me, and in her quiet manner said, "I did not know that God was in real estate."

In time, Jan became seriously ill and passed away. Ben was devastated. His presence at the café became less and less frequent. Not too long after Jan passed away Ben himself became ill. He sold his home and moved in with his daughter. When he died, his funeral and burial took place on Mackinac Island. Ben's lifelong friend gave a heartwarming eulogy after which we all went to the cemetery in horse-drawn carriages.

When the graveside services ended, we walked over to Ben and Jan's burial site. On the stone that identified their final resting place was engraved, "This is a Grave Situation."

Herman Candler

There appeared at the café on a regular basis in the late afternoon a short, stocky, slightly bent-over man. He always had books, magazines and newspapers in hand. In time we learned that he was a retired country school teacher. Many days in late afternoon our daughters would be settled in the back booth doing their homework after school. Mr. Candler took note of this and told me he was willing to tutor them. I told him I did not think they needed special tutoring. They were doing quite well in school.

One day, however, Mr. Candler came in with workbooks on math and English and headed right to the back booth. I saw him standing in front of them, giving them instructions and telling them he would be back in a few days to see how they were doing. Of course, there were protests. "What are you doing to us? We don't need this. Who is he?" our daughters complained. I tried to explain to them that Mr. Candler was a retired country teacher who probably felt the need to be needed. "Just go along," we said explaining that there was no harm, and bless them—they did go along with the tutoring. But in a short while the whole program petered out. Mr. Candler's efforts became sporadic. He would pick up their workbooks, and several days would go by before he would return them. Many times he would forget to pick them up—much to the relief of the girls.

One summer we experienced an unusual series of hot, humid days. Such sultry weather was not typical for our area. On one such day our delightful waitress Marge was standing at the cash register. Looking out the window, she quickly said, "My goodness, here comes the great white hunter." Sure enough, crossing the street toward the café was Mr. Candler in a light-weight, short-sleeved shirt, tan shorts, white socks up to his knobby knees and an armful of the typical array of reading material. On top of his head perched a large, white pith helmet. From that day on we always referred to him as the "great white hunter."

Another time Mr. Candler came in out of a heavy downpour. He was wearing a bright yellow rain slicker along with his pith helmet. He stood in the middle of the floor and tried to unzip himself. Mr. Candler was having a difficult time, struggling as he tugged at the zipper. We could hear Mr. Candler's mutterings of frustration. Georgia offered to help him. This was not easy, but through their collective effort they finally managed to free him of the slicker. Of course Mr. Candler's glasses were wet. He asked Georgia if she would clean them for him.

76

This was the beginning of a ritual. Rain or shine, whenever he made his appearance, Mr. Candler would ask Georgia to clean his glasses.

Leon Bennett who owned a jewelry store next to the theatre noticed that Georgia had become Mr. Candler's official glasses cleaner and remarked that we were victims of Mr. Candler's whims. He explained that a few weeks prior Mr. Candler was in the market for a wristwatch. It took several visits and endless questions before he decided which watch to buy. He finally made his choice. The jeweler set the proper time before handing it to his customer. Mr. Candler left seemingly pleased; however, every day since he made his appearance before the jeweler and asked him to check the time to see if the watch was running properly. Was it losing time? Was it gaining? This habit became a ritual and, ironically, one could set one's watch on his daily visitations.

Every so often we would not see Mr. Candler for a few days. On telling him we missed seeing him, he would explain that he had attended a retreat in a monastery, just below the Mackinac Bridge. We wondered who checked his watch and cleaned his glasses during his absence.

One day Mr. Candler gave us a dictionary, just in case we might find a use for it. "One never knows," he said. Oddly enough, it did come in handy. Some of our customers worked crossword puzzles. At times there would be a discussion on the spelling or meaning of a word and Mr. Candler's dictionary offered the solution.

One late summer day Mr. Candler invited Georgia and me to his home, a room at a local motel, to celebrate his fiftieth wedding anniversary. "Bring your daughters," he said. The invitation and occasion puzzled us since we had never met Mr. Candler's wife, let alone known he was married. We were to be there at 7 pm. He gave us the name of the motel and the room number. We parked the car and spotted the motel room. When we reached the entrance we noticed a sign had been posted to the door. It read, "IF YOU SMOKE, SWEAR, DRINK ALCOHOLIC BEVERAGES, YOU ARE NOT WELCOME." We could not help but chuckle at this strange greeting. We knocked on the door and a cheery "come in" greeted our ears. So in we went. A tidy, neat room awaited us. We could tell immediately he was very pleased that we had come and that he was very much alone. Mr. Candler said we should wait in case anyone else should join us. We waited for several minutes. He finally resigned himself to the fact that no one else was coming. Mr. Candler served us chocolate cake and coffee and gave the girls chocolate milk. The whole situation seemed bizarre. During our visit we would discreetly ask questions, trying to avoid prying and outright direct inquiries, but slowly the story of Mr. Candler and his marriage came out. This was truly his fiftieth wedding anniversary. During World War II the Soo was inundated with some 15,000 U.S. Army personnel. Their mission was to protect the Soo Locks. Mr. Candler's wife became involved with one of the out of town G.I.'s. One day she up and left him and to our knowledge never made contact with him again. She just disappeared. In spite of the unfortunate circumstances, Mr. Candler's marriage meant something to him to "celebrate" as he did with no bitterness or recrimination. We felt sorry for him and at the same time found his positive spirit admirable.

Mr. Candler brought us much amusement over the years that he patronized the café. He was a good, kind soul whose idiosyncracies made him all the more endearing.

Smokers

There was a time in the 1950's when the high school located on Spruce Street, only a few blocks from the café, had an open campus. This meant that at noon the students could leave the school grounds for their lunch period. Some stayed at school to eat their lunches, but several sauntered downtown, many into the café and took over the last two or three booths near the basement. They would immediately bring out their cigarettes, light up and order a Coke. Some would order French fries. Their patronage was appreciated, but the small premises would fill quickly during lunch. The adults who came for lunch had bigger appetites and larger wallets, and they could not be accommodated due to the booths being overtaken by the students. I realized that our income was diminished by this arrangement. I also noticed that this lunch break gave the students freedom to light a cigarette away from school and parental disapproval.

If I eliminated this "privilege" they exercised, it would be the catalyst that I needed to eliminate their taking over much-needed space for our regular patrons who would spend a little more. After all, I was in business to earn a living. A sign was made and placed in a conspicuous spot. HIGH SCHOOL STUDENTS – ABSOLUTELY NO SMOKING – 25 CENT FINE. The sign worked, although some would light up anyway and they had to be reminded and fined. With this privilege gone their presence diminished.

In the meantime, I developed a habit of checking the lavatories after the lunch rush due to the students' frequent visitations to the basement. On entering the facilities, I would routinely find numerous unopened brown bags on the floor, every day except for weekends. The bags contained sandwiches, cupcakes, cookies and fruit—all probably prepared by their mothers. And that's where their efforts wound up—on the floor of the lavatories, unopened in favor of a Coke, fries and a cigarette. I felt very sorry for the mothers—their attempts at nourishment gone for naught.

Paul Harvey, Good Day!

During the weekdays Paul Harvey came on the radio at 3 p.m. Just prior to the broadcast, the counter stools would be filled with customers. Coffee would be served, cigarettes lit, and when Paul Harvey came on the air there was total silence. Everyone was all ears until the broadcast was finished which was followed by brief comment or discussion on what the customers heard. Then, one by one, they would depart. It was like a club. The waitresses and I would anticipate their daily "meetings".

T.J.

How and when T.J. came into our lives and became a part of The American Café clientele is hard to pinpoint. He was a quiet fellow who exuded a warm, friendly aura. As time passed and we became better acquainted, I noticed he had an innocence that was a rare commodity in the give-and-take of human relations. He did not have the capability of being employed on a steady basis, but one accepted him as he was with his even disposition and comfortable presence. He was short and slight of build. On knowing of his lack of work I hired him to help after closing for the day. He put items away, swept the floor, mopped and tidied the area.

During the 1950's and 1960's the local health department, through the powers of the State, insisted that all food handlers were to be given tests for tuberculosis. One could not work unless they passed the test and in doing so would be given a card they had to keep in their possession. Whenever the health inspector came for his periodic inspections we had to show him our card. This included T.J. He went for his test and shortly after was told he had tuberculosis. We had to release him and arrangements were made to send him to Marquette to a sanitarium. There he stayed for over a year. Every so often we would send him care packages. Brief notes from him acknowledged these and told us of his activities, which did not amount to much from what we gathered. The first few months were devoted to rest, sleep and very little physical activity. Toward the end, however, he was introduced to woodworking and crafts. When he came home he presented our daughters with attractive and well-constructed jewelry boxes which they still have. When he left he was thin, and on his return over a year later we did not recognize him. He had gained so much weight that when he walked, he waddled with great effort. It was apparent he was well-fed and the lack of activity had done its work in defeating his tuberculosis.

I re-hired T.J. when he was able to work. He also began to receive some remuneration from the state. This was of great help to a man who, otherwise, would have been destitute.

About this time a house-to-house retail service came to the Soo as it probably did in many communities. They specialized in household needs and had a variety of holiday specials throughout the seasons. This was Jewel-T and it appealed to the housewife who was unable to leave home to shop freely. T.J. also found Jewel-T very handy and became quite addicted to this service, especially during Christmas.

Christmas Eve at the café was a pleasant affair. After spending hours and extra energy serving and providing for our customers was an event we all looked forward to: we would lock the doors in mid-afternoon, gather around the back booths after cleaning up the café and treat ourselves. Many of the waitresses would bring in their culinary specialties; we would exchange gifts, chatter and reminisce and finally bid each other the usual warm holiday greetings and leave for our homes. Of course some of the waitresses would have their husbands or boyfriends join the party. The drinks were on the house.

T.J. was not a drinker; at least not a habitual one. Once in a while a cold beer would replace his usual coffee. He never smoked, but he developed a habit of using snuff and this was obvious when one could see quite noticeably his lower lip protruding beyond its normal size. For some reason he also developed the habit of drinking "boilermakers"—a shot of whiskey ingested in one full swallow followed by a glass of beer. I could never understand how anyone could possibly enjoy this combination. In my mind a whiskey should be sipped slowly and far from having any beer before, during or after. To me, this invited trouble.

One Christmas Eve, T.J. sat at the counter and made himself at home with the festivities surrounding him. In the meantime he was casually taking in his boilermakers. His usual intake

81

was one of each and that was it for the day. On this particular Eve I noticed he was on his second drink. I did not think much of this since we were all enjoying the goodies to nibble on, gifts to open and pleasant conversation. An hour or so later we began to wind down the evening, ready to head for our respective homes. Then someone said, "Where's T.J.?" We all looked around, but he seemed to have disappeared. Suddenly someone pointed to the foot of the stool where he was all crumpled up and said, "Here he is!" He had overdone his boilermakers, and without a sound he must have slowly slithered to the floor in a heap. He seemed quite comfortable in his position, but he was out cold. Efforts to wake him were fruitless, so two of the big fellows carefully unfolded him and carried him out to their car. He made not a murmur, not a peep, as they took him home. One of the fellows remarked when he returned to get his wife, "We poured T.J. into the car and we took him home and poured him into his bed." To my knowledge T.J. never ordered a boilermaker again.

In the middle of Christmas afternoon a ring on the doorbell announced T.J.'s arrival at our home. He would come by cab with bags of unwrapped Christmas gifts. He was most generous to our little girls. He seemed to know just what would tickle little girls' fancies, and, needless to say T.J.'s arrival on Christmas Day became anticipated with great zeal and excitement. He joined us for Christmas dinner and this continued for several years.

T.J. was a great fan of the television program "Bonanza." The day after the evening's performance, he would come in and ask if we saw it, and he would review in his mild, simple manner the highlights. One day I noticed that a fan club had been established for Lorne Greene, an actor who played the father role. I asked T.J. which of the characters he liked the best and he said all of them, but Lorne Greene was best of all. I sent the fan club T.J.'s name and address and mentioned his fondness for Lorne Greene. From that time on he would receive news bulletins from the fan club regarding Lorne Greene's movies, travels, hobbies and interests. Whenever he received any fan mail, he made sure we knew about it.

T.J. did not have much to keep him interested. His education was limited and so were his interests. He would sit at the counter for great lengths of time over coffee, fondling the end of his nose as if he had a comfortable, pleasant pre-occupation with this pastime. He would then leave and not too long a time later he would return and spend more time just sitting. One day I asked, "T.J., do you ever get bored?" He looked at me for quite some time and then, in a quiet monotone voice asked, "What's that mean?" I didn't have the heart to explain. I just smiled and told him I didn't know either.

One day an illness hospitalized him. He never recuperated. We lost a quiet, gentle and unforgettable man.

Mr. Slope

Whenever the Dial-A-Ride bus stopped in front of the café we anticipated the arrival of Mr. Slope. He was a tall, slender man in his late 70's. He walked slowly, with what appeared to be a tired gait. He looked as if he had experienced a long, hard life. We soon learned that he was a widower who had farmed for a living, and because he was no longer able to perform the daily demanding duties that a farm required, he had decided to sell his place and belongings.

He would sit at the counter quietly smoking his favorite cigar. The particular brand he favored was sold in compact packages of five. I believe they were called R.G. Dun Tiparillos. We sold them, and he was one of the customers who purchased them on a regular basis. One other customer who favored this slender cigar was the owner of a jewelry store. He would buy four packages at a time, where Mr. Slope would purchase one package at a time.

One day there were no cigars available for Mr. Slope. The jewelry store owner had bought the last packages. Mr. Slope was upset and remarked that we should have more on hand, since now he had to walk to the corner where Callaghan's Grocery store was located. On his return I mentioned that the cigars he favored must be quite special since we had similarly-shaped cigars made by other companies.

"Those won't do," he exclaimed. The ones he favored were the best because they relieved his painful arthritis. I could not fathom the relationship between smoking a cigar and the medicinal benefits of relieving arthritis pain. In time we managed to learn more about Mr. Slope's weird sense of, shall I call it, humor.

Mr. Slope came in one afternoon for his usual coffee and cigar. The waitress noticed that he had an unusually large ring on his right-hand index finger. The ring, she said, had no stone or gem in it—just a plain ring that at one time might have held a large stone. It was apparent he was gesturing with his hand more than usual. The waitress asked if he knew that his ring had no stone. He responded that he knew and added that it was the best kind of ring one could have. When asked what he meant by that, he said he could wear that ring and not have to worry about losing the gemstone; it freed his mind of that concern. He felt liberated by such a notion.

We had never seen him wear eyeglasses until one day when he had them on. No one remarked about this until it became apparent that the eyeglasses were just a frame—no lenses. When this was brought to his attention, he paused for several seconds, as he always did before answering. Finally, he said that he discovered he could see better without lenses. Everything was clear. He wore these lensless frames for several days. Then once again he came in without them.

One afternoon our waitress, Mary Anne, finished her shift and called for the Dial-A-Ride to pick her up for a ride home. When she came to work the next day she told us that when she boarded the bus she saw Mr. Slope sitting with a small TV on his lap. The early TV sets were usually encased in an artificial wood cabinet. The one Mr. Slope held on his lap was in a yellow plastic case. Mary Anne struck up a conversation with Mr. Slope and asked him if his TV set was a black-and-white set or a colored one. He took a thoughtful moment before answering, looked at her and said, "Offhand, I'd say it was yellow."

The Soo was experiencing a long and dreadfully cold winter one year with much snow. One afternoon Mr. Slope came in for his usual coffee and cigar. After a long silence he asked me if I would like a newborn kitten. I assured him I would not, that I was not a cat lover. Again a long silence, and then he stated that his cat gave birth to six kittens a couple of weeks ago. He had asked many people if they would like one—free. No one wanted a kitten. He said he did not know what to do since his living quarters were very small and he had no room for them as they grew. He did want to get rid of them. Without thinking and in a joking manner, I suggested he put them in a bag, tie the top of the bag and place the bag out in a snow bank some night. He said nothing, finished his coffee and cigar, and he left.

Not too long after, we were hit by a severe snowstorm. Traffic, vehicular and pedestrian, was practically at a standstill. Several days passed and once again life came back to the stranded city. In came Mr. Slope. He sat at the counter as usual. For quite some time he was totally silent. As I passed him our eyes met and I acknowledged his presence and commented on the weather. Then he said that he did what I told him to do. Time had passed, and I did not remember what I had told him. He refreshed my memory when he told me that he put the newborn kittens in a sealed bag and put the bag out in the snow one night. "They sure were stiff the next day," he said. After that sobering moment, I never volunteered any suggestion to him about any dilemma he admitted to having.

One summer in the late afternoon the Dial-A-Ride bus was unable to care for its passengers. It had broken down. Mr. Slope told us it was a good four-mile walk to where he lived. I told him I could drive him there. He accepted, and my daughter Joy came along with us. He had difficulty getting into the car. His long legs, afflicted with arthritis, made it challenging. Following his directions, we came to his home on a dirt road. It looked like a shack, constructed of a hodgepodge of multicolored boards and metal sheeting. He invited us in. We were stunned to discover his floor was a dirt floor, totally bare of carpet, rug or boards. A small bed stood at one corner. A small table and two chairs were in the other corner. A small sink and

85

an ancient yellowed refrigerator noisily chattered in the other corner. One bare light hung from the ceiling. The walls were covered with newspapers and posters of every description. A large, fat cat slinked about, staring at us in a suspicious manner. There were no toilet facilities—just an outhouse behind the ten-by-ten shack. We exchanged a few words, and we left. Joy and I were speechless and totally humbled by what we saw.

When we sold the café, contact with the delightful people who were our patrons came to a halt. Rarely would our paths cross. One day, some years later, I delivered flowers to a resident of a nursing home. It was summertime. As I approached this facility I saw several of its occupants sitting on lawn chairs under the extended marquis over the entrance. I did not recognize anyone, but suddenly I saw the tall, slender figure of Mr. Slope with a cane in one hand, and a pipe in the other.

I greeted him, happy to see him. He looked up, stared as he usually did, and a faint, mischievous smile greeted me; pleasant memories of an unforgettable character. A dear man.

Mr. Ball's Garage Fire

Vern Ball was a good friend and steady customer of the café. He and his wife, Bea, owned Co-Ed Flowers and Gifts, a small shop on Ashmun Street. They were hard workers and quite devoted to their venture and family. One day Vern came in to the café, and with his coffee in hand proceeded to tell me of his father's adventure the previous day.

A policeman had stopped at Vern's shop to ask where Vern's father, Bill Ball, was. He needed to inform Bill that his garage was on fire. Vern told the policeman that his father was having coffee at the coffee shop in Kresge's Department Store. The policeman hurried over to Kresge's and found the senior Mr. Ball enjoying his coffee and smoking a pipe. The policeman told Mr. Ball about the emergency, anticipating an excited or hysterical reaction. Mr. Ball hesitated a moment and then asked the policeman if the fire department was on the scene. "Yes," replied the policeman. Mr. Ball sat back, continuing to smoke his pipe, and then confidently remarked, "Well, the fire is in good hands, there's nothing more I can do," and he took a sip of coffee and sat back to enjoy the rest of his morning.

This man lived for 104 years.

Fasting

Any business, small or large, is always grateful for regular steady customers. The café was blessed with regular patronage from the employees of the neighboring department store, Montgomery Ward. Some 35 men and women worked there and many came in for coffee and a Danish or coffee and a cigarette before going to work. Others came in during the day on their break, some for lunch and a few for a beer or two after work and before going home. Even though we locked the doors at 9 p.m., the "gang from Wards" always managed to persuade us to reopen, and in no time three to five booths would be filled with the store's employees. There are endless stories regarding these delightful people. Besides being a great source of our income, they created a bond as an extended family.

One of the ladies employed there was Meg. She was either a widow or a divorcée. She had a son and daughter. When the last day of the work week came, she would approach my father and remind him that it was Friday and she wanted assurance that the soup of the day was meatless. My father was conscientious about this; he informed her that Friday soups were always meatless. Nevertheless, Meg posed the same question every Friday. For lunch she would have soup and a tuna salad sandwich.

Friday night as the Montgomery Ward clan gathered, Meg would make her appearance and she would order a beer with the rest of them, mostly men. Her consumption was stimulated by the beer treats, the gaiety of the group, and most frequently at the end of the evening, she would be in such a stupor that the fellows had to drive her home. The thought came to my mind then as it does today—how could she be so adamant about honoring her meatless fast on a Friday and yet have no qualms about getting as "drunk as a skunk" that very same night?

Mushrooms

I had not seen one of my regular customers, Fred, for several days and on inquiring I was told he was sick in the hospital. He had to have his stomach pumped because of some poisoning. When he finally recovered and returned to the café, I asked him what had happened. Fred told me he had gone mushroom hunting with his parents as a youngster and was very familiar with "good" and "bad" mushrooms. He felt quite confident in this activity and never had a bad experience.

One day not too long before, Fred went to his favorite mushroom area and gathered a good crop. He looked forward to getting home to fry his mushrooms in butter as he had done for years. His wife was away, so the whole process was in his hands and he relished every morsel of his morels. Late that night he experienced painful stomach cramps. He was not getting any relief no matter what he tried, so he decided to go to the hospital emergency room. Fred was admitted and before he knew it he was having his stomach pumped. In a short time he felt relief from the mistakenly picked, cooked and eaten species of inedible mushroom. While recovering he was fed intravenously, so he was looking forward to a real meal. After two days of abstinence from food due to mushroom poisoning, the hospital served him a bowl of cream of mushroom soup.

Fred's final remark after telling me of his gastronomical adventure sums up my own reaction to hearing it: "Can you imagine?"

The Ferries

Before the bridges were built between the two Saults (Michigan and Ontario) and at the Straits of Mackinac, the traveling public and commercial vehicles relied on ferry boats. Ferries crossing the St. Marys River from one Soo to the other accommodated both people and vehicles. Ferries crossing the Straits of Mackinac were enormous. One of them handled the tremendous weight of passenger and freight trains. The other transported vehicles of all sorts: passenger cars, trucks and buses. In the summertime these ferries were taxed greatly. Vacationers invaded the Upper Peninsula from the Lower Peninsula and vice versa. Many times the traffic traveling to Soo, Ontario, was so congested that the vehicles had to line up and wait their turn. During the busy summer months these waiting periods were an hour and even longer.

I recall one traffic backup from the Soo ferry dock located next to the Coast Guard Base on Water Street all the way to The American Café, a distance of approximately five blocks. Many people took this in good stead, but a few others became angry and temperamental. In those days air conditioning had not reached the Soo, and on hot summer days our small café would be like an oven. Even fans were minimally helpful.

On one such sultry day our café was jammed. My father and I, cramped in our little kitchen, were trying to keep up with orders as best as we could. The heat did not help. Our waitress told us that an elderly man was complaining about the slow service and kept pestering her. Periodically he would turn his head toward us and make angry gestures. Seated in the same booth opposite him was a young couple. They appeared somewhat calmer, but as I glanced up in their direction I sensed they were upset with the older man and were trying to quiet him down. In the meantime the waitress tried to assure him that we were doing the best we could and asked him to please be patient.

The old man continued to harass the waitress. In a burst of anger, I left the kitchen and went to his booth. I had no idea what I was going to say except that I was upset with him and his attitude. As I stood there in front of the old man, I asked him, "How old are you, sir?" He angrily retorted "Sixty-five!"

"Well," I said, "If you have had the patience to arrive at such a nice age, surely you could find enough patience to wait to eat. My father and I are doing the best we can."

"Hey," the man said, "We have to catch the ferry. We are on vacation." I walked away to finish preparing their food. They stayed, ate, paid and left.

This whole affair bothered me for quite some time. One day, as I walked past the Central Methodist Church a sign caught my eye. The church was and remains today on the corner of Spruce and Court streets. Facing the public, the church had a large sign that presented a clever, thought-provoking message along with the time of services and the minister's name. This particular week the sign read:

"IF YOU ARE TOO BUSY TO GO TO CHURCH,
THEN YOU ARE TOO BUSY!"

I dwelt on this thought for quite some time. I felt it was a good message and had much value. Then one day, recalling the impatient man's anger and frustration and his muttering about ferry schedules and vacations, I came up with this variation on the church's message:

"IF YOU ARE ON A VACATION AND ARE IN A
HURRY, THEN YOU ARE NOT ON A VACATION!"

When we planned our new menus, which we did every spring, I had this message printed on them. I was pleased at the reaction of the traveling public. Many vacationers would express their appreciation for the thought and promised to abide by it. We oddly never encountered impatient customers from that time forward—a real blessing in the restaurant business.

The Inspectors

Just as soon as Halloween ended the merchants began their Christmas preparations by hanging holiday decorations and displaying seasonal merchandise. Thanksgiving came and went with a mere nod being lost in the glitter and glamour of the impending Christmas season. As the season progressed, Christmas carols were so frequently played in the stores and on the street loudspeakers that they seemed to lose their meaning.

I put off decorating the café for the holidays until two weeks before Christmas. With wreaths around each booth sconce and garland hanging here and there it admittedly changed the ambience considerably and helped revive my holiday spirit.

The two weeks before Christmas were a constant stream of activity downtown—like one huge family on a spending spree. Business was brisk from first thing in the morning until closing which was late at night.

One evening in the midst of a busy supper period, I found myself up front by the cash register. My mind was on the business at hand, taking cash and glancing up and down the booths and counter hoping all was caught up in the kitchen. A man sitting on a stool at the counter asked me, "Do you have a liquor license?" I thought that was a strange question. I hurriedly answered, "Yes!" A brief moment of silence passed, and he asked, "Where is it?" This, too, struck me as a bit weird. I quickly replied, "Hanging on the wall behind me!" To this he said, "I don't see it."

He must have sensed my questioning expression together with frown and frustration. He pulled out his wallet and showed me a badge. "And what does this mean?" I asked.

"I'm the liquor inspector for this area while the regular man is on vacation, and I'm checking things over. By the way, your liquor license is covered, and it should be exposed." I looked up and noticed a bit of garland had been accidentally draped over it. "Oh," I replied, "It's the Christmas season, and in a couple of weeks all this will be coming down."

"Can't wait for two weeks," he commented. "I suggest you do it now." And I did. I wondered to myself—why couldn't this man with his badge have been more civil? Couldn't he have introduced himself in a pleasant way at the outset, instead of using his authority in such a heavy-handed and condescending manner?

Six months later, summer was creeping up on us. I realized our ice cream sales had slipped considerably. I thought it time to do some promoting. I decided to have a special on banana splits. With each split we would give a free fishing lure. A couple of ads in the paper, an attractive display in the window with bananas and fishing lures, and a brief announcement on the radio and we were ready to go. On the morning of the day we were to feature this banana split special, the phone rang and a man said, "I see you are giving away a fishing lure with each banana split today."

"Yes," I answered. "Come on down and have one." The voice responded, "You can't do that." I replied, "What are you talking about? I'm just trying to promote my ice cream sales." The voice responded, "Peter, this is Hank. When you have a liquor license you are not allowed to give anything away. It's against the State Liquor Commission Law."

"But what has ice cream got to do with beer and wine? Besides, if we can't give anything away what about the matchbooks we give away free every day?" I asked.

"You are not allowed to do that either, so you had better cancel this banana split promotion. Don't do it," he responded.

The only way I could notify the public immediately was to have the local radio station make spot announcements throughout the day. We had some patrons come in for the split and lure promotion, but we had to explain the situation and to appease them I gave them a fishing lure sans purchase whether the liquor inspector liked it or not. Nothing more came of this, although it was embarrassing.

Not all of the state health inspectors were as "gung-ho." Many were considerate and dispensed helpful information. But one in particular became a thorn in my side. With his clipboard in his hand and stern sober expression, he had a habit of quickly running his tongue around his lips before uttering a word. His reputation was such that whenever he appeared in my competitors' places of business, the owner would call me and tell me that Nester was in the area. I would always return the favor. Whenever Nester walked in, he would slowly move behind the counter and stare for endless moments at the malt machine and the glasses. Then he would lift the covers of the ice cream bins and stare at the ice cream for several seconds. Then he'd wander to the sink area and place a thermometer in the water and a slip of paper in the disinfectant bin to measure the strength of its contents. All of this investigation was legitimate, of course, but I found Nester's method frustrating, making me wonder what was going through his mind.

The café had two areas for washing, one for dishes, pots and pans, and another area strictly for glasses. This setup was perfectly satisfactory for many years. Inspectors would come and go and none uttered any complaints. One day Nester stood before this arrangement, staring and scheming, until he finally called me over and suggested—demanded—that we install another sink for washing our hands. The area was so small I couldn't perceive a sink that would fit, and I politely told him so. His answer: "Find one!" A plumber friend located one and it was installed. The whole affair made no sense to me, since washing dishes and glasses was a matter of immersing one's hands in hot, soapy water and having both them and the glasses cleaned in the process.

Nester always made it a point to come in the middle of a lunch rush. One day he stood and watched me slice tomatoes. He suggested I use a fork to pierce the tomato instead of using my hand to hold the tomato. I nodded my head but continued doing it my way. As I did, I looked at him and said, "Think about it. Wouldn't that be a bit awkward?" He stood for a brief moment and walked away.

Whenever he went down to the basement he seemed to be gone a long time. I often wondered if he were suffering from constipation or diarrhea. After one such prolonged basement visit Nester came up with his ever-present clipboard and asked me to come downstairs with him. Into the back storeroom we went. For years we had placed boxes of supplies directly on the cement floor. Nester insisted I build shelves on one wall and wooden slatted platforms to store the boxes on, instead of directly on the floor.

I did what he asked. Six months later Nester returned. I followed him downstairs curious to get his reaction to my compliance with his previous request. Again Nester stood and stared at the platforms. Finally he said I should put wheels on the platforms, so that they could be moved about. Years later, as I reflect on Nester's insistence that I have a platform built for the supplies, I believe he had a good point. If any water managed to leak on to the basement floor, it would have caused quite some damage to my inventory. With the wheels in place, the platforms could be moved for cleaning the floor and the inventory would be preserved. Nester's manner of imparting these requests, though, still rankles me.

The one inspection tour that will remain in my mind forever is the toothpick incident. Nester had finished his tour and had made copious notes on his clipboard. As I looked up from the kitchen eagerly awaiting Nester's welcome departure, I saw him staring at the end of the counter where we had a display of gum, Lifesavers, candy bars and other small point-of-purchase items.

I watched Nester pick up a toothpick and place it in his mouth. As he did so, he grabbed several more and put them in his shirt pocket. He called me over and pointing to the small glass holding the remaining supply of toothpicks, Nester said, "This is not a healthy situation, these toothpicks." "What's wrong?" I asked.

"Well, people coming to pay could cough, sneeze and contaminate the toothpicks, and spread germs," Nester explained.

I nodded my head, and away he went, sucking on a toothpick with a shirt pocket full of "contaminated" toothpicks.

Not too long after this criticism I discovered that toothpicks were available as individually-wrapped units. Mint flavored, to boot. Straws also were now available individually wrapped. These innovations must have made Nester unfathomably happy.

The Watch

A few days before Christmas one year, one of our customers sat at the end of the counter contemplating a list with pen in hand and a beverage nearby. "You look quite serious," I commented. "Is that your Christmas list?" He said it was and that he was trying to decide whether he should give one of his sons a wristwatch for Christmas. The lad was in junior high.

He remarked that at first he thought it would be a great idea. But the more he thought about it, the less he liked it. "You know," he said, "as we grow, our lives become controlled by time. We become clock watchers, and we lose some freedom because of this obsession with time. I think I'm going to forget the watch for him and think of something else. Time will capture him soon enough."

The List

Over the years I had developed a habit of making lists to help me remember what to buy for the café and what to repair or do around the store and at home. Many times a day I would note that I was running short of food items or other products that were needed. I would list the items and where to get them as well as note any equipment that needed attention. I kept the lists in the kitchen, and as the day progressed I would quickly jot down the items that came to my attention. There were quiet times when I would sit on the stool at the end of the counter near the kitchen with pen and paper, nursing a cup of coffee. Many times I would leave the list on the counter for short times when I had to see to something else that needed my immediate attention.

When I wasn't occupying the stool, a customer would sit there, sip his beverage, and chat with the waitresses or me. One of the regulars made a point to favor this area. One particular day when I was in the midst of making my list, I also had orders to prepare in the kitchen. I left my perch and as I did, I also left my list on the counter. That evening as we cleaned up in preparation for the next day and as I was about to close up to go home, I looked for my list. I found it where I had left it. On looking over the list my eye ran down the entries and the last item I saw, not written in my hand, was the word "sex."

At first I was discomposed, shook my head in disbelief and then found myself expressing a faint smile. I shrugged my shoulders and headed for home. The next morning about the time the Ward gang came for their morning coffee break, one of the young men came up to me in the kitchen and called my name. As I looked up he smiled and said, "Well?"

Bagpipers

One summer day I could hear the faint strains of a bagpipe drift through the open door. I thought I imagined this until a customer came in and told me there was a bagpiper coming down the sidewalk in full Scottish attire. Bagpipes excite me, but being too busy in the kitchen I could not run out to witness the performance.

As it turned out I didn't have to go anywhere, for as the sound of the bagpipes grew louder the bagpiper entered the café, playing with great gusto. The sound reverberated extremely loudly in the confines of the small space. With the bagpiper were a young lad and lassie who were also dressed in traditional Scottish attire. I assumed they were his children.

It was a warm day and I instructed the waitress to give them a cold pop to drink. They drank and thanked us, but before leaving they hesitated as if waiting for something. It was quite some time later that it occurred to me that the piper would have liked some monetary gift. After all, he had given me a gift—a concert of my beloved bagpipe music.

The Pitcher

One busy summer day during the lunch rush, a young man came in and stood in the middle of the café. He was motionless muttering unintelligibly. I had seen him around town many times walking the streets, but he had never entered the café. As he stood there we wondered just what his intentions were.

He was an obstacle to the waitresses as they maneuvered around him to wait on customers. He made no move to take a seat. He just stood, stared ahead and continued to mutter.

Then, as if he were a mechanical doll that had been wound up, he went through all the gestures of a baseball pitcher in action. His arms began to move as if he actually had a ball in his hand. He warmed up and with a loud grunt pitched the imaginary ball. As he did so he stood still and stared toward the imaginary batter at home plate. The pitcher would then make a facial gesture of either satisfaction or disappointment.

This went on for several minutes. Shortly these antics caught all the customers' attention. Finally the pitcher shrugged his shoulders, turned, and walked out. The customers returned to their food. We continued with our duties. The pitcher never returned to "pitch" in the café, but he was seen walking the streets daily.

The Cigarette Machine Man

Many years ago I asked Georgia to give me some ideas of what she would like for Christmas. She did not hesitate. She said she would be happy and pleased for only one gift—that I would quit smoking.

Anyone who is addicted to cigarettes knows how difficult it is to quit. In past years I had tried to stop, but to no avail. I admired and respected her request. Georgia was concerned for my welfare. Could anyone find fault with this? In the past, I had failed her. That Christmas season, however . . .

One late winter afternoon not too long after Christmas, I ran out of cigarettes. I went to the cigarette machine which was located in the front of the café right next to the entrance. The only occupants in the café, to my knowledge, were my waitress and me. It was a typically quiet winter afternoon.

I placed my coins in the machine, selected the brand I favored at the time and bent over to pick the pack up. As I did, I felt a tap on my shoulder. I was startled and looked up to see a rather pleasant man. He had a tanned complexion and penetrating blue eyes. He smiled at me. As we stared at each other he said, "I just want to tell you, as one human being to another, you are killing yourself." He tapped my shoulder again gently and left the café.

I asked the waitress if she had seen the man. Because the café was so small, I was quite aware of all the people in it. The waitress said no and remarked that there was and had been only the two of us.

Not too long after this "mysterious stranger" episode, I quit smoking. It wasn't easy, but I believe whoever it was who tapped me on the shoulder that day added some years to my life. Georgia received her belated Christmas gift.

I feel compelled to record something I read some time ago. I do not remember the person or the source, but I believe it relates to my cigarette experience:

"For a long, healthy and happy life, listen to your wife!"

The Discount

After so many years of relatively equal value between American and Canadian money, the Canadian dollar began to lose some of its worth. Banks began to discount Canadian money. At first the majority of the Soo, Michigan businesses absorbed this difference, but in time, the disparity became so great that many businesses began to charge the extra on Canadian currency in the same manner as the local banks. I decided to follow suit at The American Café.

Many American tourists returning from trips to Canada would pay for their meals or purchases with the Canadian money they had accumulated during their Canadian journey. Just about every one of them would complain and some would argue vehemently at this monetary loss. Many accused us of benefiting from this charge by upgrading the status quo. I found these insults unjustifiable. It was difficult to try to explain the situation and that it was not of our doing especially during busy periods with people waiting and duties to perform. What to do?!

I finally made a sign and posted it on the cash register facing the customer. It read:

"THE DISCOUNT ON YOUR CANADIAN MONEY IS THE SAME AS THAT CHARGED BY OUR LOCAL BANKS. IF YOU HAVE ANY COMPLAINTS, PLEASE CONSULT THE ECONOMIC EXPERTS—NOT US. THANK YOU!"

There continued to be a few complaints but not as many as before. In fact, this message provoked some humor and grudging acceptance of the fact—minus the mean-spirited verbal hassle.

Canadian Holidays

The café enjoyed good Canadian patronage from our neighbors across the river in Soo, Ontario. This was quite obvious on Fridays, and especially on Mondays. When a Canadian holiday came along—and there were many throughout the year—it would always be observed on a Monday.

There was one friendly fellow who came into the café, sat at the counter, and had a beer or two while his wife shopped. She would join him some time later. They would then move to a booth and have lunch.

One day I remarked to him how nice it was that the Canadians had so many holidays and that they always fell on Mondays, thus extending their weekend.

"Yes," he said with a smile. "We do have a lot of holidays. If the queen farts we have a holiday." He let out a boisterous laugh, raised his glass and said, "God bless the queen. Long live the queen!" and he ordered another beer.

The Canadian Bookkeeper

Every so often at lunchtime the Dial-A-Ride bus would stop in front of the café and a tall, slender man would emerge and amble in. He always wore an English tweed short-brimmed hat. He would sit at the counter and regularly order a bowl of chili, brown toast, no spoon, but a fork. He was toothless. The slim fellow managed to eat a small amount of the beans and meat with the fork.

"Slim" would tip the bowl to his mouth with the remaining broth, as well as dip his brown toast in the liquid. When he was given his guest check he would remark every time that he was from Canada and that he was a bookkeeper. Through his thick-lensed glasses he would peruse the guest check for a long time.

Near the entrance we had about four stacked chairs to be used by customers seated at the ends of the booth. One day he took one of the chairs, placed it in the middle of the floor, removed his shoes then his socks, rubbed and massaged his feet, replaced his socks and shoes, and walked out.

Time passed, his patronage became less frequent until we realized that we did not see him anymore. In spite of the bookkeeper's idiosyncrasies, we missed him.

The Boss

One day a mother and her young daughter, Sarah, came in, sat in a booth and ordered while they waited for their husband and father to join them.

I remembered my father had a long-standing habit of giving youngsters a candy cane, a sucker, or some small treat. I tried to continue this tradition, so after the mother and daughter settled down, I approached them and offered the little girl a sucker. She was about four or five years old. Upon receiving it, she immediately began to un-wrap the sucker. Her mother said, "Sarah, aren't you going to thank Peter for the sucker?" The little girl continued to un-wrap the sucker and didn't acknowledge her mother's request.

"Sarah, did you hear what I said? Thank Peter for the candy." Silence. "Sarah," repeated the mother, "Thank Peter, or he will take it away." Silence. "Sarah, if you don't thank Peter he will never give you candy anymore."

Silence, and then in a loud, commanding voice Sarah looked up at her mother and said, "You thank Peter. You're the boss."

101

The Ca-Choo Club

The Soo has always been noted for its clean, fresh air and its freedom from pollen. For many years the Soo became a haven for those who lived in Lower Michigan, Ohio, and Illinois who needed an allergy-free environment. Their native areas were polluted with pollen from early summer until fall. Many people would come to the Soo for relief. In fact, one of their number organized a loose group and called themselves the Ca-Choo Club. Many "members" would come and stay for the season.

One of the apartments over the stores in the Soo Theatre building was reserved for two ladies from Toledo, Ohio. The pollen count in Toledo was high and intolerable for those sensitive to it. The two ladies would stay until the pollen season changed. These ladies were unique in that they both wore black from head to toe. They also wore wide-brimmed straw hats. These hats were also black.

In time we learned that the shorter of the two was a wealthy spinster from Toledo. Her family owned a large, successful department store. Her companion, just slightly taller, was her handmaiden. They were always together. They patronized the café periodically. Their favorite time was late morning for breakfast. The shorter of the two did all the talking.

She had a deep husky voice that reminded me of the famous actress of that time, Tallulah Bankhead. When she spoke, you listened. Her authoritative voice matched her commanding appearance. Through our conversations I concluded that she was a hypochondriac. On asking her how she felt each morning, she would expound on her sleepless night, or her splitting headache, or her upset stomach. It was always something. Then she would utter a husky chuckle with an, "Oh, well."

We would miss seeing her for several days and when she made her appearance, we would mention that we had missed her. She would respond by telling us she was in bed all that time and not at all well.

Their breakfast order was always the same: one poached egg in a bowl and whole wheat toast. They regularly specified that the egg not be served on the toast but in a bowl. One morning the waitress cleared off their table and discovered, lying next to the bowl, a small child-sized spoon. The spoon handle had an ornate design on it with the letter "A" engraved at the top. As we were admiring it, the phone rang.

It was "A" calling, in a state of panic. Had we found a spoon? We told her we had. She sounded relieved and told us her companion would pick it up. She also said it was given to her when she was an infant and she treasured it, she always used it and took it with her wherever she went.

Another morning I happened to clear off their table. Hiding under a napkin, I discovered a small bottle containing an amber colored fluid. Looking at the bottle I concluded that because of her health condition perhaps it contained a urine specimen. Not being busy at the time, I decided to take it to her.

I went to the apartment and knocked on the door. Her voice came through, loud and clear: "Who is it?" I responded, and she opened the door. She was pleased to see me. I told her I had something that I thought belonged to her and handed her the bottle, wrapped in a napkin. "Oh, dear, oh, dear," she exclaimed. "Now you know my secret. Every morning for years, I take a tablespoon of bourbon before breakfast. It's a real tonic, you know. And Peter, if you should be interested in bourbon, buy the cheapest. It's all the same and the best bargain is Dover Bourbon."

I could not help but tell her what I thought—that the bottle contained her urine to be tested at the lab. Her laugh, coupled with embarrassment, was mingled with several exclamations of "Oh, dear, Oh, dear." She extracted a promise that I would not tell anyone about her bourbon. And I never have—until now.

Snowstorms

I saw the beginning of a snowstorm one night but assumed that by morning it would subside and all would be back to winter normality—whatever that is in Sault Ste. Marie. Not so. The storm had continued through the night and greeted us in the morning. I still felt compelled to go to work. It was a struggle wading through the deep snow in high, rubber boots. When I finally arrived at the café and made preparations for the day, I realized that no one was going to work downtown that day.

Roads and sidewalks were impossible to travel, and I felt I had made the wrong decision in trying to open the café. I should have stayed home. The waitress called to inform me she could not make it to work.

But suddenly people began to come in and in a short time the café was completely full. I was overwhelmed. I was told that the power had been interrupted, and there was no electricity in the surrounding area except for our block. People could not make coffee or cook breakfast, so they came to the café.

I called Georgia out of desperation and she came to help me. To this day I wonder how she was able to maneuver her way through all that snow. By late morning, near noon, we were exhausted. We were close to running out of food. The stream of customers had dwindled to practically nothing. We closed the doors, cleaned up and went home.

On one other wicked winter morning I managed to walk to the café. Streets were totally impassible for both cars and pedestrians. Again I found myself alone. The waitress was unable to make it in to work. An hour or so went by and not a soul appeared. Suddenly the door opened and a father and his son of about 10 years old popped in. The winter storm was intense, snow was blowing every which way and winds were howling. Visibility was so bad that one could not see across the street.

Father and son looked like walking snowmen. They were covered from head to toe with white powder. In spite of their condition, they were laughing and enjoying every minute. After they managed to brush off the snow and sit down, I approached them for their order while we talked of the storm. Of course, the young lad was elated. "No school!" he exulted.

I anticipated an order for a hot cup of coffee and hot chocolate. They surprised me greatly when they ordered chocolate ice cream sundaes. When they finished their desserts, they ordered two more. This was a special celebration of a joyful day without responsibility. I admired their adventurous spirit and their beautiful father-son relationship.

The Mirrors

Large mirrors on the wall faced the customers sitting on the stools at the counter. I have often thought how intriguing and amusing it would be if these mirrors registered what they reflected and played back the scenes of human conduct, perhaps like the video cameras of today. My mind has "recorded" many of the mirror images, and I "play" them here. Reflect on this . . .

The Mustache

In the 1930's and 1940's men took great pride in their moustaches. They were always neatly trimmed and waxed, and those who sported handlebar moustaches would sit on their stools, twisting and shaping them endlessly. As they did so, their expressions in the mirror reflected pride and a sense of pleasure.

Toothpicks

Many men would have a toothpick sticking out the side of their mouth and there it would remain—even in conversation. Others would pick at their teeth endlessly, and many of these men would look at themselves as they cleaned the toothpick to see what they had loosened. When satisfied, they would drop the bits and shreds on the floor, the counter, in their cup or saucer, or in an ash tray. One man, I recall in particular, would pick at his teeth in a discreet manner. He would use one hand to pick and with the other hand he would cover his mouth as if he did not want to be seen picking them, although the mirror reflected it all.

Tears

One man I remember especially well came in with a sober, serious look and sadness seemed to fill his countenance. As he sipped his coffee, the mirror reflected the tears slowly running down his cheeks. They were silent tears. Several minutes passed, he left his money on the counter and walked out.

Faces

Another man seemed to find pleasure in having his tongue circumnavigate his lips. Slowly, round and round his tongue would circle the perimeter of his mouth for quite a length of time. Others would wink at their own reflection, first with one eye, then the other. This was followed by a shy smile. Many would make faces at themselves, from smiles to grimaces—a whole series of expressions reflecting back at them as if they were "testing" them for future use on others. The ladies found the mirrors a reservoir of pleasant reflections while adjusting their hair, their earrings, moistening their lips and reapplying their cosmetics.

Cigarettes

Several patrons who smoked seemed to find pleasure in watching themselves light their cigarette, inhale deeply and exhale slowly through their nostrils and then their mouths. Many would amuse themselves by exhaling round circles of smoke and watching the rings reflected in the mirror.

Bob

One fellow had the habit of bouncing up and down the very moment he sat on the stool, At first his bounces would be slight and slow. As he sipped his coffee his bounces became more intense. As he did so he smiled, staring in the mirror in a hypnotic manner. We called him Bouncing Bob.

"Hey, Pete—Your Café is on Fire!"

The landlord said that our fire insurance costs could be reduced by a new program that he had learned about. Since we both had the same insurance agent for fire coverage it would be worth looking into. An appointment was made. I met with the agent and the owner of the agency.

The theatre building complex where our café was housed had other retail businesses downstairs and apartments upstairs. The café, using gas and electricity for cooking and food preparation, was subject to a higher rate in fire insurance premiums. The agent explained that the cost could be lowered by installing a new fire alarm system over the cooking area: the stove, the grill and the fryer. In fact, this special system was later to become mandatory for all businesses and institutions that were involved in commercial cooking.

The insurance rate would be reduced upon having the new alarm system installed. Up until that point all we had, and all that was required, was a fire extinguisher on the premises. This was handy as long as there was someone available to use it at a time of need. The new detection and alarm system was functional all day every day and was automatically activated should a fire start.

It all sounded reasonable and I soon learned from the building inspector that it was a necessity if we were to continue operating the café. Arrangements were made to have the new system installed. The company that sold and installed this system had a monopoly over the entire Upper Peninsula. It was located in the extreme western end of the U.P.

A large red box was installed on the wall and pipes ran across the edge of the hood that covered the stove, grill and deep fryer. From these pipes six shower-like heads extended over the cooking area. We were told that should a fire begin the heat would release a chemical that would be sprayed over the cooking area, thus smothering the fire. The chemical sprayed was non-toxic, easily cleaned up and would not be harmful to the cooking surfaces.

In due time we learned that the fire insurance rate was reduced; however, when the full picture of this new development came into focus, the reduced rate became a farce. The cost of the unit and its installation amounted to hundreds of dollars. Then we were told that the unit had to be tested four times a year by a technician. He had to be paid $20 to $25 each visit. The testing amounted to no more than five to ten minutes. The door to the "gadget" was sealed by a wire and a tab. The technician would cut the wire, remove the tab, open the door, push a button or two, and release a small handle that would emit a loud, snapping sound. He would then close the door, install a new wire and metal tab and present a bill. As time passed, these service calls would increase in cost until they reached just about double the original fee.

Fortunately we never had the experience of having a fire, thus we never learned how well this system worked. However an incident occurred that was shocking and frightful.

A year or two had passed since this new alarm system was installed. One day the mailman approached me with a large registered envelope which required my signature, thus confirming to the sender that I had received it. On opening the envelope, I found a letter directed to me personally describing the contents and, in a tactful manner, insisting that I pay special attention to the importance of the new feature of the fire system that was recently developed.

Sophisticated diagrams and related literature accompanied the letter implying the importance of this "improvement" and how superior it was to the one we had. The cost was exorbitant: close to $1,000 as opposed to the initial system's cost of $400 to $500. I couldn't see the reason for this upgrade. I tore up the envelope and its contents and dropped it in the garbage can. A few weeks went by and this communication was forgotten.

One afternoon the phone rang. It was a call from the fire prevention equipment company. I was asked if I had received their registered envelope, and I assured them that I had. The response was a question: When could they come to improve the system with their new state-of-the-art creation? I told them I could not afford such an investment. I had girls in college and that was our priority. Besides, the system we had was functional, and I saw no need for such an upgrade.

The man was adamant that I reconsider, and he said he would call again in a week or two. I assured him that was not necessary since I had already given him my answer. His final response was, "Think about it!" Several days later he called and again I told him I was not interested. Without a goodbye or friendly farewell, he put the phone down.

Some weeks passed. We were in the midst of a busy tourist season. One night during the early hours of the morning, the phone rang at home. We were all fast asleep. The phone ringing at that hour was startling and frightening. I answered it and I heard a loud male voice in a panic stricken immediacy. "Pete! Pete! Your café is on fire!"

I slammed down the phone. I was overwhelmed. At that hour the news was devastating and shocking. The whole family was awake. The girls were crying. I dressed immediately and told Georgia I was going to run to the store or take the bicycle. She insisted she go with me in the car. We quickly arrived on the corner of Spruce and Ashmun streets. Our café was in the middle of the block on Ashmun, easily visible from this corner.

At that hour the city was fast asleep, no traffic, no sign of any life. As we arrived at the corner a quick glimpse showed us nothing—no cars, no fire trucks, no police cars, no smoke— nothing but silence and emptiness. We parked the car in front of the café. As I placed the key in the door, I could see everything was clean and clear. There was no smoke and no sign or indication of a fire. We checked everything, from the basement to the main floor. Nothing. We returned home, and tried to get back to sleep. We were relieved, yet confused.

Daylight came. The café opened for business. The activity kept me occupied enough that I did not dwell on the disturbing event of the night before although periodically it would enter my mind. At the end of the day I decided I should report the incident to the police. On the way home I did.

The desk sergeant listened and told me I should have

called them or the fire department first (who can think clearly under these circumstances?). Then he remarked that it was a good idea that I did not go alone in case it might have been a plan to have me appear by myself. Whoever planned this could have attacked me, where they would hesitate with two persons being there. All well and good, I thought. His summation sounded like good common sense.

The days passed. The event also began to diminish in its impact. However, the more we talked about it, and the more analyzing we did, we began to suspect the fire prevention equipment company—if not the company, then perhaps one of its overzealous salesmen wanting to frighten us into installing that new fire extinguisher. We have no proof of this, but our conclusion made sense to us. Man, in desperation, is capable of anything.

Several days passed. One afternoon the phone rang. The waitress told me someone wished to speak to me. It was a male voice inquiring if I had made a decision, because their crew was coming to the Soo to install some new systems. I immediately went into a tirade, telling them what they did was a dirty trick and that I wanted nothing to do with them—ever. That finally ended the blazing affair.

The Drunk

The story of the Good Samaritan is important for it shows the abundance of mercy that may come from the least likely of persons. It takes place in a treacherous rural landscape, on a dangerous road, where thieves were common. Samaritans, though Jews, were not considered so: they followed ceremonies differently than the establishment.

Yet the Samaritan is the sole person who demonstrates compassion and mercy to the victim abandoned on the road. He helps a man he doesn't even know. Out of love alone he helps and saves the man's life. The Samaritan's love is real and practical, not some concept.

How far the cultural apparatus of the tale must appear from our lives: the oil and the wine the Samaritan pours on the traveler's wounds; carrying him to the inn; ensuring the man's continued care by paying for his needs before continuing his own journey. Most of us recoil in disgust at the other passersby. We, at least, would call an ambulance. Who of us would fail to ensure the care of such a victim?

Jesus wants us to know that every person is our neighbor, is our brother or sister, worthy of our attention, compassion and mercy. If ever we are to imitate Jesus' love, we must remember no one is outside our circle of concern.

– Forward Day by Day

Keeping a café clean is an endless task. Many of these cleaning projects had to be done after business hours. Many times I would be just too tired and anxious to get home to my family to stay once we closed for the day. I did the minimum, then left. Consequently, the "deep cleaning" duties would pile up.

One of the cleaning projects was time-consuming. Our beer cooler faced Ashmun Street and from there I could see all the activity going on outside. Over a period of time, bottles of beer would break, spilling their contents into the base of the cooler. Whenever this happened, we would do our best to pick up the broken pieces and clear the immediate area to prevent any cuts and accidents from broken glass. In the meantime, beer would remain on the bottom and the odor became quite noxious. At that point the bottles and the metal partitions of the cooler had to be removed and the bits of broken glass picked up, the stagnant liquid on the bottom of the cooler mopped up and the whole interior washed down, dried and reassembled.

One sunny Sunday morning when the café was closed for business in early spring I found myself in the midst of this unpleasant project. Woolworth's across the street opened its doors on Sundays at noon. Around 11:45 a.m. a few people would gather waiting for the store to open. Looking outside, I saw a group of boys standing, waiting. Suddenly one of them pointed to something on our side of the street but just beyond my vision. He seemed excited and gestured to his companions and they all trotted across. I became curious, left my project, stepped outside for a better view and noticed a small crowd around my car. This naturally caught my attention and I quickly moved toward the scene. When I reached our car, I saw a man with his hands on the hood, bent over. There was blood on the hood and bumper. I recognized the injured man as one of the "town drunks". Before I could react in any way a police car came by and took the man away. The crowd dispersed and I stood there staring at my car with the blood on it. What happened to the man to cause him to be injured and bleeding, I never did know. I do know that I found myself cussing the drunk and going into the café for a bucket of soapy water, a brush and rags. I was relieved that there was no apparent damage done to the vehicle—only the blood to be cleaned off. I felt no sympathy for the man, just anger and disgust. My concern was for the car, not for him.

As the days passed, I saw the man staggering in a stupor, passing by the front window. A month later he made the obituary column. He was in his late 30's. He was found dead behind an alley in the center of town.

I was the complete opposite of the Good Samaritan at a time when one was so desperately needed. This incident happened many years ago, and I still dwell on my selfish response and heartless behavior.

Catsup!

I had just started down the driveway at our home when I felt an uncomfortable pain in what is referred to as "the great right toe," the large toe in my right foot. Each step bordered on excruciating. To drive the car for one block to avoid the painful walk seemed to me a waste of fuel and an admission of non-endurance. "To hell with it—I'll walk," I thought.

I blame catsup – ketchup, whatever you want to call the bloody liquid, for the discomfort. And it happened some 30 years ago at the café.

I was quite proud of the gravy I made. Judging from the great number of hot pork and hot beef sandwiches we served, the public thought the gravy that accompanied them was tasty. Many orders of French fries would come in with a request that gravy be poured over them. But then I would witness the "great insult". Some of my customers would request catsup and they would pour it all over my gravy. Catsup would also be used to smother eggs and hash browns, bacon, ham and sausage. One woman was insulted when the waitress brought her the customary maple syrup and butter. She insisted on catsup, "and take that stuff away," she exclaimed, pointing to the syrup. The abusive use of catsup galled me. There were many times when dishes that had contained French fries would come back without fries but full of an enormous amount of catsup. In my opinion, with the overuse of catsup, food lost its identity, its own unique flavor.

One day I discovered we needed to fill the catsup containers. Because of the lack of space in the café proper, the majority of our supplies were kept in the basement storage area. I remember going up and down these stairs as often as ten to twenty times in just a few hours. So down the basement I went and picked up two arms full of supplies among which was a #10 tin of catsup. This container is larger than a coffee can and about five times as heavy. I took two or three steps up, and then suddenly the tin of catsup fell from my collection of supplies and dropped on my foot. The pain was sharp, instant, and brought tears to my eyes. I managed to get upstairs and limped the rest of the way to the kitchen. This was after the noon lunch rush. The pain did not diminish.

At closing time I limped home. The pain kept me up all night. The next day was no better, so I went to see Dr. Scott. X-rays revealed a cracked bone in my "great right toe." I was given painkillers and told to keep off my feet. One cannot run a café with the prescription of "keep off your feet." To do so would mean simply locking the doors and staying home until the wound was healed. A shoe added to the discomfort, so I wore a slipper for several days. In time, all went back to normal.

As the years went by, however, I found it necessary to seek the services of a podiatrist. In seeing my feet, he noticed my great right toe had developed a strange bump and was malformed. He said I should have the foot in a cast, and he cautioned that in time arthritis could develop in that area. Indeed it has. I'm on my feet a lot, there are things to see and do, and vegetating on a comfortable chair (unless I am reading or eating) is not the way to see and do them.

While some days are less painful than others, I continue to struggle in overcoming the curse of that bloody, vile liquid—catsup.

Feet on Seat

The booths my father and uncle purchased and had installed in their new location in 1930 were made of solid oak. They once had a beautiful silver-grey finish. The oak stood up well, but over the years the finish became worn and lost its rich patina. In 1961 we decided the booths should be refinished.

About that time we became aware of a product that was durable and colorful. The new product had to be sprayed on and was said to wear well. It also had a pleasant, tweed-like pattern to it. One of the main ingredients was lacquer.

On applying the new finish, the highly concentrated lacquer gave off a noxious odor that was difficult to cope with without getting overwhelmed. In fact it was so penetrating that the odor found its way into the theatre and its patrons were "victims". Although no one became sick, the unpleasant odor was obvious, and we were told about it. The painters had to take frequent breaks outdoors for fresh air, even though the front doors were kept open during their work. The final job gave the booths, and the whole café, a new and fresh appearance. This lasted a few years. Eventually it had to be done again.

Our regular customers had developed a habit of leaning back and placing their feet on the seat opposite them. This was much like sprawling out on one's favorite couch at home, but in this case, with one's shoes or boots on. We accepted this since we felt it was pleasant to know they felt at home and comfortable. This homey habit continued, even after we had gone through the cost and trouble of refreshing the booths.

I was reluctant to tell the customers that the rules had changed, not wanting to offend my good clientele. I was naturally quite concerned about this and perhaps the old adage of "necessity is the mother of invention" came into play. I made little table signs and placed them in each booth. The message on the signs read:

"SHOES ON FEET LOOK NEAT –
BUT FEET ON SEAT NOT SO NEAT!"

– Confucius say

It worked. The customer's lounging habit stopped and the booths were used as originally intended. Best of all no one, to my knowledge, was offended.

115

The Men's Store

One winter, we were experiencing an extended run of below-zero weather. Early one morning, Joe came rushing into the café in a state of anxiety, harried and angry and asked me if I could give him a pail of hot water—quickly. Noting his disposition, I did not inquire why he needed it, but did as he asked. He ran across the street with the pail.

Joe was the son-in-law of the owner of a popular men's wear store downtown. It was Joe's duty to open the store in the morning. He was conscientious and industrious.

A few minutes later, Joe returned for another pail. I gave it to him and away he went. He eventually returned again with the pail in hand, sat down at the counter, lit his cigarette and ordered his coffee.

Joe had by now become composed, and he told me that when he went to insert the key into the door to enter for the day's work, he noticed that someone had urinated on the lock and handle. The mess had frozen solidly during the night's sub-zero temperature. The frozen liquid was quite apparent on the lock, the door frame and doorway. The hot water apparently helped.

Joe was a Marine during World War II, and I've often wondered what he would have done to the culprit had he known who he was.

On another occasion, my shoelaces had broken on both shoes over a period of a couple of days. I was too busy to replace them, and I managed to tie the ends so that they functioned in some way. One morning, these repaired shoelaces broke again. I finally decided I had better take time and remedy the situation. I ran across the street to the men's shop and told Joe I was in need of a pair of shoelaces. Some 20 minutes later I returned to the café with a new pair of shoes. Joe was quite some salesman!

Pepto-Bismol Days

One February brought us endless days of severe, bitterly cold sub-zero weather. Week after week, windless days saw the thermometer hover between 15 and 30 degrees below zero. Pedestrian traffic was practically non-existent. Unless it was an emergency, people hesitated to venture outside. On one of these days, I discovered I needed napkins to carry me over until I could order a case of them from my supplier. I hurried down the street to Scott's Department Store. Streets were empty and so was the store except for a few employees. As I entered I saw the manager, Henry, lifting a bottle to his mouth, and I recognized it as Pepto-Bismol. I asked Henry if he was all right. Henry was a tall, nice-looking man with a pleasant manner. He shook his head and told me he had gotten a phone call from his headquarters and his overseer was upset because store sales for the month of February were too low. The supervisor was adamant and threatening and insisted that Henry do something about his sales. Henry tried to explain the weather conditions and the reason for the drop in sales. This was not the first time Henry had received this type of call. He said ever since the bitter winter conditions came and sales had fallen, he was pestered by these superiors. They did not understand and did not want to try.

Henry went on to say he was being sent merchandise that was not conducive to the Eastern Upper Peninsula of Michigan. Just because it went well in other parts of the country did not mean it would do as well in the cold north. I knew Henry was a conscientious, industrious man and well-liked in the community. It was not his incompetence that caused the drop in sales but rather the winter conditions. This large chain folded not too much later. I believe in part because of some remotely-located moguls sitting in their comfortable, plush offices, interested in charts and graphs and overlooking the human element.

At any rate, Henry was not long unemployed. He was immediately hired by a large, stable institution where he remained until he retired and I expect his need for daily consumption of Pepto-Bismol was greatly reduced.

Yo-Yo Usher

In the beginning, and for many years along the way, the Soo Theatre had ushers to help the movie-goers to their seats and keep order, whenever necessary. The ushers were young high school students. Some would come to work earlier than their shift started and would stop in the café for a Coke. As time went by, Coke began to gain popularity with the addition of flavors added by squirting a "shot" of syrup from the soda fountain otherwise used to flavor sodas and milkshakes. This was the origin of the "cherry coke". One combination was the "suicide" Coke which entailed a "shot" of each fountain flavor into the Coke—chocolate, strawberry, cherry, lemon and root beer. It was a sickeningly sweet, unidentifiable concoction.

As the movie of the night progressed, I recall one of the ushers would regularly sneak into the café with his yo-yo. This young man was extremely skillful in handling a yo-yo. He could control it and do with it as he willed—over his head, between his legs, right, left, and along the ground. He loved to demonstrate his skill. He would enter the café and walk up and down the length of the store with his yo-yo spinning in all directions. Most of the time he'd be in front of the waitresses interfering with their work as they took orders and delivered food.

As much as we all enjoyed the young man's performance, my father could see a disaster in the making. The yo-yo exhibition could not be allowed to continue. My father would approach the usher and in a loud voice tell him, "You go home now!" The usher would turn to my father, and with a big grin would respond, "Yes, Chris. OK, Chris," and as he was leaving would continue his yo-yoing. The admonition did not discourage him. The next evening he would return and repeat his performance. Again my father would repeat his command, "You go home now!" The usher would give the same response.

Years went by. World War II came and went. One day, as I was walking on Ashmun Street, I heard a loud, clear voice from across the street. "Hey, you go home now!" It was the yo-yo usher. He had returned safe and sound from the service and was pursuing law studies in Lower Michigan. On the street, in supermarkets, in gatherings we hailed each other with this greeting and laughed. On his graduation from law school, and after passing the bar, he established himself in the Soo and practiced law, eventually he served as a judge. Whenever we ran into each other over the years we would shout out the command, "You go home now!"

He has passed away, and I believe that he is "home" now.

The Hypnotist

One late afternoon before the theatre opened its doors to the public for a visiting hypnotist, a couple of ushers came out with a large tub and placed it on the edge of the sidewalk near the curb. They then began to fill the tub with water. This tub of water created considerable curiosity, and the hypnotist drew much attention to his show.

The theatre was filled to capacity. The time had arrived and the master of ceremonies lavishly introduced the hypnotist. The curtain was drawn and out came the hypnotist dressed in a tuxedo. When the applause subsided he asked for volunteers. He needed six and six responded. The hypnotist asked for silence and undivided attention.

The curious theatre patrons complied, and the hypnotist began his program. Two of the volunteers could not, or would not, be hypnotized. The other four came under the hypnotist's spell and the first two volunteers were dismissed. When the hypnotized patrons had reached a certain stage, the hypnotist

119

put them through a series of fascinating instructions and the patrons responded.

The grand finale finally arrived. The hypnotist told those under his spell that there was a fire on the floor, that their feet were getting warm, their shoes were on fire, and that soon, very soon, their feet would become unbearably hot. In no time the four hypnotized victims were jumping up and down as if their shoes and feet were actually on fire.

He then told them the only way they could put the fire out was to run off the stage and down the aisle. In front of the theatre there was a tub of water and they were to jump into it. This they did with no hesitation. As they ran down the aisle they were followed by the audience in a near stampede. Out they went, headed for the tub, and jumped into the water. In doing so they awakened from their stupor and stood totally confused.

In order to get a better view, some of the younger, more agile and excited spectators jumped up on the hood of a car that was parked in front of the café. The car was brand new, only two months old, the first automobile ever purchased by our family since my father had arrived in this country. When all subsided to normality and the public dispersed, I went up to the car and saw that the fender and the hood were dented and scratched. Our new car was a victim of the hypnotist's power.

A Harbor in the Night

Across the street from the Montgomery Ward store was the "Booth Block", a large building that had several retail stores on the street level and apartments above. The Montgomery Ward store was a northern neighbor of the Soo Theatre complex.

One cold windy night in early spring, a fire broke out in the Booth Block. The wind was severe, coming from the east. As the fire gathered strength and began to reach the upper stairs, the wind whipped sparks. Flaming debris and gusts of fire began to threaten the buildings across the street.

Because apartments above the theatre were occupied, the fire department sent a couple of their firemen to warn the occupants to vacate immediately which they did, in their pajamas and bathrobes. That is, all but one woman. She lived with her husband in the first apartment. She refused to leave in spite of her husband's pleading and the firemen's warning. She insisted on putting on her makeup and getting dressed properly along with her jewelry. I know this because during the early hours our phone rang at home. It was the Red Cross informing us of the fire and asking if we could open the café and make coffee to accommodate the apartment residents and the firemen. Our small café was filled with the pajama-clad victims.

Firemen would come in for hot coffee and a brief spell. The temperature was below freezing for I recall icicles hanging from the firemen's helmets and even from their chins. There is something special about neighborliness in times of trouble. We were glad to be able to host this slumber party when the community needed us, in spite of the hour and the cold.

The Theatre Apartments

Friday nights were extremely busy, especially at supper time. One such Friday, in the midst of heavy activity, I could hear a thumping noise over my head. One of the apartments occupied that area. The sound would continue for a few minutes, there would be a pause, and then it would resume. It became annoying, but I was also concerned that whatever was causing the sound was also causing damage somehow.

I was too busy to pursue my concern, but when the activity in the kitchen diminished, I decided to find the landlord and report it to him. When I told him about the thumping he came into the kitchen with me and listened, and he decided to look into it. Upstairs to the apartment he went. He was gone for several minutes. When he returned he told me, "You won't believe this. I went to the door of the apartment, heard loud noises from inside and rapped on the door. No answer. I rapped louder. No answer. The music was too loud. I tried the doorknob, and the door was free to be opened. I opened it slowly, and then I saw a young couple wearing nothing but briefs. They were taking turns jumping up and down on a pogo stick. They were startled, as was I, but they promised to lower the music and stop their bouncing."

I chuckled to myself with amusement and relief. That must have been a sight.

Competition?

Before the downtown was fully developed, the empty lot across from the café had a large billboard and a small building which was the headquarters of one of the cab stands. Many times going to work or going home, I'd cut through the lot. One day the local paper informed the citizenry that this empty lot had been purchased by the F. W. Woolworth Company. The business already had a store in the next block, but they wished to expand. This was fine, I thought. It would bring more pedestrian traffic and thus help business at the café. Then the article stated that it was to have a restaurant with a seating capacity of 118. Here I was with a small café of only 40 to 45 seats. This behemoth was going to destroy us, I thought. How were we to cope with this intrusion?

Construction began and every day I would glance at the progress across the street and worry about the impending doom of our small café. At the same time I hoped that we could somehow survive with the new competition. Pedestrian traffic would certainly increase and if their restaurant would fill up, we would get the overflow. By the same token, if we were to be filled with forty or so patrons, the rest would probably patronize the Woolworth facility. This was exactly what happened. Years passed and we survived. In fact, in time the Woolworth

Company began to eliminate many of its branches, including the one across the street.

One day just before the new Woolworth store opened there appeared a young man dressed in a business suit, trim and proper, displaying all the characteristics of an executive. There he was with a small ladder and a measuring tape. I saw him at about 10 a.m. and periodically I would glance out the window to see what he was up to. He must have spent over an hour measuring the exterior of the window; on his ladder, down his ladder, stepping out to the curb when safe from traffic out on the street. With tape in hand the young man made measurements and with a marker made a mark on the window. It was truly a puzzle to me as to what he was up to with all the care and precision of his endeavors. Finally, about an hour later, he left. Shortly I saw him with another man inside the store with a huge banner in their hands. The sign was hung up and it read, "Grand Opening."

Well, I thought, this young man took all this time and effort to put up a sign that a teenager could have done in a snap. Apparently, the young man was an up and coming executive.

Through the Window

Looking through the café window over the years, much was observed. The comings and goings of shoppers, the changes in the seasons, new construction and growth in the downtown area, years of parked cars all makes and models and years when parking on Ashmun Street was not permitted, the faces of patrons as they entered the store or passed by engaged in conversation. So much of the world was happening outside of our window while we managed the little world inside the café.

Parades were one such recollection, often the only chance I had to see them was through the café window. For many years, every holiday prompted a parade. To me one of the highlights was the regular participation in the parades by a group from our sister city, Sault Ste Marie, Ontario, across the St. Marys River. I say this with all due respect to the other participants. The Canadian group was the Sea Scouts comprised of young lads from eight years old to teenagers. They were always dressed in their naval uniforms of dark blue, white caps and canvas putties or leggings. Besides their sharp appearance, what impressed me was their smart, precise marching. All in step, all eyes straight ahead, heads erect, arms in cadence and in rhythm and an apparent pride appeared in the whole group. One could see their pride, and one could sense it.

Another Canadian parade group was the Scottish bagpipers in all their glory, kilts and plaids. One could hear them in the distance like a small wave or stream slowly meandering, gathering momentum, and as the seconds blended to minutes their unique sound penetrated the atmosphere and thus the soul—I could feel the blood coursing through my body, heart accelerated and pounding. As a "wannabe Scot", I felt a pride and, at the same time, an odd nostalgic feeling would overcome me, sometimes inspiring a deep emotion and tears. Just as they passed with the smart, precise steps of the drum major and his troop, the stirring sound would slowly blend into the distance. To me there is something about the bagpipes that feeds the mind, body and soul.

The Squirrel

It was a splendid morning and consequently I had the front door propped open welcoming the fresh spring air. One of my first customers came in and sat in the booth near the back, facing the door. I gave him his coffee and joined him for a moment with my back to the door. A few moments later, the customer excitedly pointed to the front door and told me that a squirrel had just run in through the open door. As he announced this I caught a glimpse of a large grey squirrel running swiftly past us and straight down to the basement. We ran after it, but it was nowhere to be seen. He had to go to work, and I had to get the café up and running for the day. This was on a Friday. In those days the stores remained open until 9 p.m. and customer traffic was steady until closing. Whenever I found a few spare minutes, I would run down the basement stairs, check everywhere, stop and listen for some noise that might reveal the squirrel's whereabouts, but with no luck. I was concerned that customers using the washroom facilities in the basement might be harmed or frightened if the squirrel made its presence known. All day long I checked, and still there was no sign.

Nine o'clock came and it was time to clean up and go home. But I was disturbed, thinking of the damage that animal might create once we all left if it had the run of the place. I could not leave with this menace on the loose. A few doors down the street the pharmacist was preparing to leave for home. I caught him in time, however, and told him of my dilemma. He suggested poisoning the animal, and he showed me a tube of some poison. He suggested I cut up small squares of bread, squeeze poison on the pieces and spread them on the floor in the basement and also on the steps. I followed his directions precisely and left for home reluctantly and praying for the best. My sleep that night was not a deep one.

When I opened the door of the café I did so slowly, stepped quietly to the light switches, turned on all the lights and listened carefully. Silence. Then I heard a patter as if one was striking his hand on a table, at times in quick succession, then after a pause, it resumed. The patter was coming from the kitchen. I walked slowly toward the kitchen, listening, anticipating God only knows what. I could hear distinctly the intermittent patter coming from behind the garbage can. I moved the can carefully, slowly, and there on the floor lay the squirrel on its side, its eyes closed and its bushy tail beating the floor. As I stared, his tail activity diminished to total stillness. No sign of life. The squirrel left this world and a careful assessment of the whole place, upstairs and downstairs, revealed no damage. I was relieved on discovering this and yet saddened to witness and be a party to the demise of an innocent animal.

Monkey Business

The first apartment we lived in after our marriage in 1960 was a small, narrow one above the old Soo Co-op Grocery Store; then located on Ashmun Street south of the Soo Theatre. Our apartment had only two windows—one facing Oaka Alley and a small window in the kitchen facing the roof of the theatre.

Late one morning, Georgia called me at the café. Work and home were just a few steps away. She called to tell me excitedly that she saw a monkey hopping across the roof of the theatre as she looked out the kitchen window. My immediate reaction was one of surprise, disbelief and wonder. What did Georgia have for breakfast? What imagination she must have! A monkey! A live monkey in the Soo!? "Come and see for yourself," she said. I did and she was right. I saw a monkey swiftly running all over the rooftop. Not knowing what to do I decided I should inform the owner of the theatre building. As I approached the theatre, I saw the theatre owner Joe and his son Charles looking up and down the street as if they were searching for something. And indeed they were. They were looking for a monkey that had escaped from its cage. The monkey in its cage was delivered to the Soo Theatre that morning. It was to be put on display as a promotion to advertise a movie that was filmed in Africa. Somehow, the monkey managed to escape. Retrieving it was an adventure in itself.

I told them that Georgia had discovered the monkey on the roof. Joe and Charles ran up to the roof and as they did so I remembered a large fish net I had in the trunk of our car. I retrieved it and brought it up to them. It came in handy. Shortly after, they netted the monkey and managed to get it back into its cage.

This event turned a typical day in the Soo into a bit of an adventure. Once the monkey was caught, the adventure was over. Rather disappointed, I went back to my usual "monkey business".

Memorable Greetings

When asking Henry, "How are you today, Henry?" he would respond, regardless of the time of day, or any day, "As fine as frog's hair!"

On greeting Ike, who made his appearance during the morning hours, "Top o' the morning to you, Ike!" He would respond in a jolly tone and with a toss of his hand in the air, "And the balance o' the day to you, sir!"

One spring, a few days after Orthodox Easter, the door of the café opened, and in a loud voice a man shouted in Greek, "Hail Countryman, Christ has risen!" The response is always, "He is Truly Risen" which I automatically exclaimed. I looked up in surprise to see from whom this traditional Easter greeting came, and there was a tall, husky man with two companions walking toward me. He had black curly hair, an olive complexion and spoke with a thick Greek accent. I'd never seen him before. It turned out that he had heard from Paul Andary, proprietor of Ely Men's Clothing Store, that a Greek man owned the café across the street. The Easter greeter informed me that he was a paint contractor from Ohio who was there with his crew to paint the International Bridge. He was pleased to learn that there was a fellow Greek in the vicinity that he could greet in the customary Easter manner.

One of our regular customers, Jim MacInnis, lived several blocks from his feed store which was located in the downtown area. Jim walked to work and, once or twice a week, he would open the door to the café as he passed. In a loud voice he would announce the number of days until Christmas. Nothing more. Nothing less. A wave of his hand, and away he would go. Those who knew him smiled and shook their heads. Those who had no idea of what his announcement meant would look perplexed for a moment, and then continue to eat, drink, talk or read. The announcement was always welcome.

All the Montgomery Ward employees were unique. They each had special characteristics that, over time, became endearing and memorable. Whenever I was able to find a quick break I would try to sit or stand and chat with them. Nick Roberge, who always had a pleasant disposition and spoke in a quick manner, was frequently accompanied by friends and much laughter would result in their companionship. One day Nick asked me if, during my Army service in World War II, I had ever heard of a certain expression, "Listen carefully," he said, "La Foo Ja Ming!" It sounded like something from the Far East, but it certainly was not familiar to me. He said he heard some G.I. utter this phrase, and he had no idea what it meant, nor where it originated. Nick liked the sound of it and would utter it just for the fun of it. I assured him that I had never heard of this expression, but I too found it, shall I say, enchanting and fascinating.

Every time Nick entered the café he would call out, "Hey Pete, La Foo Ja Ming!" and I would reply in kind.

One of our young customers and his wife were anxiously waiting for their firstborn. When their little girl finally came, the proud new father entered the café and announced the good news with a broad smile. He then remarked that he brought his wife eleven roses. "Eleven roses?" we asked. "Why eleven?" He responded, "My wife is the twelfth rose!"

A Note of Gratitude

I think of waitresses as ambassadors. They are the personal link between the proprietor and the customer. It takes a lot of patience, understanding, and tolerance to effectively respond to the needs, whims and variety of personalities in human nature.

A great many of our waitresses were instrumental in our customers returning again and again. I never underestimated their influence. Our waitresses were like family. I felt that they did not work for me, they worked with me. I take this opportunity to thank them for the pleasant memories they provided and their contributions to creating a successful café.

Milwaukee Waitress

Summer was just around the corner and the summer tourist trade was near. We were short a waitress, and for some reason none were immediately available. Since we served beer and wine, the help had to be 18 or older. One afternoon a woman in her late 20's came in to apply. She was just in from Milwaukee and needed a job. She had worked in restaurants all her adult life, she said, and she liked it. She was taller than my father and me, and had a strong, healthy look. We asked if she could start the next morning, and she happily agreed. When she started and became acquainted with our operation, she caught on quickly. She had a ready wit and was pleasant with the customers, efficient, and all in all, she was well-liked. My father and I learned a whole new restaurant lingo and expressions we had never heard before working with her. One of the first utterances, as she hurriedly passed the kitchen was, "Wreck two, three strips, two brown!" We were dumbfounded. I asked her what she meant by, "wreck two." She was surprised we didn't know her restaurant code. "Oh," she exclaimed, "that means scramble two eggs," she gave us an odd look and scurried away. Not long after she passed the kitchen with "Adam & Eve on a raft!" "What's that?" I asked. "That's two poached eggs on toast," and again she gave us a look of wonder. Later on I learned that she had worked for several years at a truck stop outside of Milwaukee where she learned the jargon.

She was with us until early fall. Little by little, she told me how she'd had an argument with a boyfriend in Milwaukee. She liked him very much, and she never revealed the cause of their estrangement, but she was hurt enough that she decided to board the Greyhound bus and get away. As the summer wore on she would, on occasion, wonder if she did the right thing.

One morning, during a busy breakfast session, I heard her voice loud and clear exclaim, "Bill!" I looked up and there was a young man, a neat, nice-looking fellow, tall and lean, a huge smile on his face. She ran up to him, paused briefly as she stared at him, and then embraced him warmly. "I knew I'd find you sometime," he said. She stayed with us for another two days. The summer trade had dwindled and our need for that extra waitress was not as strong. We missed having her diner charm, but we were glad to know that things turned out well for her— for both of them.

Betty

Another summer and the tourist trade was fast approaching. Once again we needed an extra waitress. The high schools in the area had released their students and many of them were looking for work. In came Betty, a recent high school graduate, who was planning to get married and needed work. She appeared to be bright-eyed, positive, and wore a constant smile. She was short in stature and neat. She was hired.

At that time, the Soo traffic increased on Fridays. Friday

was the day country folk came into town for their shopping. Prior to World War II, Saturday was the busy day, but somehow Friday took its place. Retail stores were open until 9 p.m. At that time I would lock the doors to the café. However, in the restaurant business, one does not simply lock the doors to the business and go home as one might do in retail stores. The café had endless odds and ends of duties, chores to do, and in many instances preparations for the next day. On top of that, the crew from Montgomery Ward gathered in for a beer or three to unwind, talk shop, and just enjoy the fellowship that was a part of their natures. They would take over four to five booths, talk and laugh, guzzle their beer and frequently stay until 11 p.m. or later. This made for a very long day.

Betty had a winning personality and an energetic disposition. She was always on the move, dusting, cleaning, polishing and talking at the same time. When her shift ended at 9:30 p.m.—which included a half hour cleanup after closing—she loved to stay and serve the Ward's gang their beer, joking and bantering with them. She enjoyed them and they her. It wasn't long before they learned that she had been a cheerleader at Brimley High School.

In those days slacks and jeans were not the norm for females. Dresses and skirts were the popular and normal attire for women, and our waitresses always wore uniforms. It didn't take much persuasion from the Ward's crowd to have Betty demonstrate her cheerleading routine. Bold, without inhibition, she went through her routine. This would end in cartwheels. She maneuvered herself to the entrance of the café and cartwheeled to the back near the juke box. In doing so her uniform would fall upward, revealing her tight pink panties and thus much of her legs and tummy. Hand-clapping and shrieks of delight would fill the small café, and again, it didn't take much to persuade her for a repeat performance. Some weeks down the road her fiancé came to pick her up after work, and that ended her entertainment. Her performance was done in innocence; it was just a part of her outgoing personality.

Lunch for my father, waitresses and me was always after feeding the masses. Activity generally slowed down by 1:30

131

p.m. and it was time for us to have our lunch. My father's favorite was a bowl of soup. He would sit in the back booth, read his Atlantis Greek American newspaper from New York and sip his soup. One day he looked up from his paper and called Betty over to tell her something. As I looked up, she was leaning over the booth table, trying to listen to my father. She let out a shriek and ran down the basement stairs. My father stared at his soup, beckoned me over, and pointed. There, in his half-empty bowl, a set of false teeth was staring at us. Betty was in the basement for a long time when she finally came up full of apologies. Aside from the humor of it all, I wondered how an 18 year old girl could have false teeth.

Shortly after the holidays she married and left with her husband for the East Coast. He was an accountant. A fine young man—reserved and quiet. I often wonder how he managed being married to a bundle of energy like Betty. Opposites attract, apparently.

Oregon Waitress

We read of abuse today in the media and we find it ever so prevalent. In the case of one of our waitresses it was my first experience. I found it devastating, and I felt helpless.

She was a tall, slender young woman from Oregon. She married a man from the Soo when he was in the service and she had a small child. She needed work desperately. I hired her, and she began work the next day. She had a quiet, slow, but thorough way about her, and she fit in quite well.

Two days after her arrival, I noticed her husband coming in at about 2 p.m. This pattern continued like clockwork. As he sat there smoking and sipping his coffee, he would lean over the counter, whisper to her, and with some hesitation, she would reach in her pocket and give him something. As the days went on, I realized he was asking for her tips and she appeared to give them to him reluctantly.

Several weeks went by and every so often I would notice black and blue marks on her wrists and arms. Once in a while she called in sick but assured me she would be in to work the next day.

One of her favorite foods was a toasted BLT with extra mayo and a Coke. Supper business had just finished one evening and she asked for her sandwich for supper. She sat in the back booth eating it. Behind the back booth there was a large mirror. In came her husband and on seeing her sitting in the back booth he went straight to her and sat opposite her. He leaned forward and spoke with her in an angry voice. He shook his fist at her and suddenly he picked up the sandwich and flung it into her face. The mayonnaise splattered all over her and the mirror. She was as stunned as I was, and she sat there motionless. He immediately stood and left. She went to the basement, cleaned up and continued to work her shift.

The next day she called in to tell me that when she was walking home the night before and passed the high school building, he had jumped out from the bushes and struck her several times and walked away. Could she come back in a couple of days, she asked, and I told her yes. She worked until the summer trade of tourists waned, gave me a week's notice, and told me she was going to try to get back home to Oregon.

The week passed, and she left. A few days later a customer told me that a 24-hour service station on the hill was held up near midnight. The afternoon newspaper came, and there was the story. The station attendant said it was a quiet night and near midnight a masked figure came in, pointed what looked like a gun at him and demanded money. The attendant complied, and as he was handing over the money the individual started to sob and apologized for her actions (by this time she'd unmasked herself) and dropped the toy gun. She said she was trying to get money to buy a bus ticket for herself and her child. She wanted to go home to Oregon. The sheriff's department was called, the story repeated and the next day money was collected from employees in the City-County Building. She and her child were escorted to the bus station and saw to it that she was safely bound for her home town. To this day I do not know

133

whatever happened to her abusive husband. I pray she arrived at her destination and that her future became much brighter than her past.

The response for help was and is a reflection of the warm empathy that Soo citizens have for those who are down and in need. I wonder if in these current times she would have been given the same pardon and shown the same mercy. I'd like to think so.

The Stubborn Waitress

One of our waitresses was somewhat stubborn in her views. For example, if a customer came in and remarked that it was cold outside, that the temperature was four degrees below zero, she would reply defiantly, "No it isn't. It is three degrees below zero." One day she claimed that hot water froze more quickly than cold. The hotter the water, the quicker it would freeze. I could not convince her. One of our patrons was a new science teacher in the high school. When the teacher came in for his supper we approached him with this question. He was surprised that such a comment would come from an adult. It didn't make sense, so he explained to her how wrong she was. She listened. When he left, after having his supper, she made the remark that she did not care if he was a science teacher. He did not know what he was talking about, and that her theory was correct.

One day after perusing the local newspaper, she informed me that the governor of Michigan had died. I had just finished looking at the paper and saw nothing of the kind. News of that nature would have been front page news. There was nothing to inform us of that, and I told her so. "Yes, there is," she said adamantly. "The governor of Michigan did die," and as she spoke she flipped through the pages. Somewhere on page six there was a small article announcing the death of the governor of Michigan Barbershop Singers Organization.

The Juke Box Waitress

Between the 1930's and the 1960's, the juke box played a great role in restaurants and bars. Even during the hard times of the Depression, people found some coins to feed the juke box and fill the air with their favorite songs of the day. One of my waitresses, a single parent raising a small child, was addicted to hearing a particular singer of the day. The fellow was in his prime, and his singing could be heard on the radio and on juke boxes continuously. Any tips that Jane, the waitress, collected would go immediately into the juke box to play her favorite singer. This was continuous during her whole shift. I often wondered why she would put her hard-earned money into this machine when it took all she had to support herself and her child. She had a passion for the singer, and it just had to be fed. Day after day during her shift we were exposed to the same singer, the same songs. One song that she played repeatedly began to wear on my nerves, and it did not make sense to me.

One day I asked Jane what she heard in that particular selection. "It's beautiful, the words, the melody—I just love it!" she replied. "Geez!" I said, "What do you get out of lyrics that keep repeating Holy Baloney?"

"Holy Baloney? Holy Baloney? Peter, that's not what he is singing. That's 'Only the Lonely.'" Needless to say, it was Roy Orbison. As I reflect on this episode, it was probably the beginning of my need for a hearing aid—although there were times that it was just as well I didn't have one.

Marge

We had many dedicated, conscientious and industrious waitresses during the years we owned the café. Most of our

135

waitresses were in their 20's and 30's. Very few were older. One day a pleasant woman applied for work. She was just a whisper in size and appeared to be in her late 50's. We were in need of a waitress. Her neatness and eagerness was most appealing, and we hired her.

Marge was a great choice. She was with us for over three years. Customers loved her and treated her with respect as well as shared with her their off-colored jokes, to which she was able to respond in kind. She lived in an apartment with her husband, just around the corner from the café. After her shift she would go home, change to smart and fashionable clothes and take her little Chihuahua for a walk. The dog's name was Chi-Chi.

Marge was the life of the party—even if there wasn't a party going on. From parading up and down the restaurant with a broom handle as her dance partner to cheerfully greeting customers and bestowing little gifts on our three daughters, she was a treasure to know.

One day Marge and her husband decided to move from their apartment, and they purchased a home in a small town a few miles from the Soo. She continued to work, but after several months discovered commuting was a bit much and she gave us notice. On hearing this, our customers all chipped in and bought Marge gifts. Cake and coffee added to the farewell festivities. A couple of years later we learned that she was diagnosed with cancer. Not long after, she passed away.

Much time passed. One summer day we decided to take a drive out past Marge's country home. Nearing their home, we saw that her husband's truck was in the driveway. We decided to stop and pay him a visit. He was very surprised to see us but pleased that we had stopped. Over coffee we reminisced about the years past, and I asked him, "By the way, whatever happened to Chi-Chi?"

"Oh," he said "Chi-Chi is up there." He pointed to the top shelf in his kitchen. "She is in that Hills Brothers Coffee can. We had her cremated."

The Bus Boy

A busy summer necessitated the hiring of a bus boy and dishwasher. A young lad whom I had seen growing up to a teenager came in for a job, and we hired him. He proved to be quick and conscientious. He did his work well and willingly. The end of the tourist season came, and I had to lay him off. A year or so later he was hired by Montgomery Wards as a handyman.

One early spring day the store received a shipment of bicycles. They needed to be assembled for display. The store had a vacant lot next to their location. Here many of their outdoor wares were displayed: canoes, boats, tents, lawnmowers, and other outdoor equipment. The manager asked the handyman if he knew how to assemble a bicycle. He said he could. He was told to put several together then wheel them to the lot for display and chain them to the fence, which he did. Late that afternoon a sudden heavy downpour hit the Soo. The manager told him to hurry and bring the bicycles into the warehouse. The young man ran out eagerly, unchained the bikes, hopped on one and began to pedal toward the warehouse "hell bent for leather," as the old saying goes.

He hadn't gone 50 feet and the bicycle fell apart. He gathered the parts, dropped them in the warehouse, and went after the rest of them. All the bicycles met the same fate. The young fellow's experience in assembling a bicycle was nil, but his eagerness to please was his undoing. Surprisingly, he was not fired.

The head of the paint department of the same store came in for coffee on his usual break and related another story regarding our mutual employee. A shipment of paint had come in. One case was damaged to the point where the cans were dented. One of the young man's duties as a handyman was to bring supplies to the various departments. When he delivered the paint to the department manager who saw the damaged

137

paint cans, the department manager told the young man that he would have to sell the dented cans at a discount.

Up to that point, the paint department manager told me, damaged paint was a rare occurrence. But soon, more dented cans were appearing. In a short time, there were more dented cans than good ones. In the meantime, this young man was buying many of the dented paint cans at a discount. The department manager strongly suspected that the handyman was deliberately denting the cans, to his advantage. Just as soon as he was relieved of this duty, the dented cans ceased to exist.

The Food Disaster

We had been married nearly three years and we had not had a vacation in all that time. Georgia's mother, who lived in Chicago, was not well. In the meantime, I had lost my father and we were blessed with the arrival of our first daughter. The Air Force Base in Kinross was in full swing. During the summer, I hired a couple of young airmen to help because of the extra tourist trade. They were fine young men, learned quickly and, although they were willing to work, their café shifts depended on the shifts they had with the Air Force.

The time came to visit Chicago and Georgia's family. We entertained the idea of closing the café for a few days. This was in late September and the tourist trade had diminished. We knew from experience that we would be facing the usual leveling off of business and diminishing income. The young men and waitresses assured us that they could handle the café. "No problem," they said. "Stay open, we can do it." They persuaded us. Before leaving I told them my main concern, although there were many, was the delivery of frozen food items that would arrive on Thursday. "Please," I emphasized, "when the delivery comes, place it all in the freezer immediately." Salesmen of frozen foods would come on Tuesdays, orders were given and delivered on Thursdays. We went on our trip and my mind kept creeping back to the café and how the employees were doing. A few days later, late at night, we returned. I took my family home and immediately took off for the café. On quick inspection all looked orderly, but when I made a trip to the basement to check the food delivery, I was greatly disappointed. All the food was sitting on the floor; it had not been placed in the freezer. Food that cost some $350 was a total loss. The next day I issued reprimands and sincere apologies were echoed.

This was an expensive lesson, but at the same time we adjusted our thinking and planning. From that time on, whenever we felt a need to have a break, instead of a mental/physical breakdown, we closed the doors. For several days before doing so, we had small table and window signs made announcing our closing and opening dates, and the waitresses also informed the customers. I was always fearful we would lose our steadies, that they would find another path and habit. Not so. We were pleased and grateful that they all returned after we did, and we even gained new customers.

BPOE

When I was growing up, perhaps in junior high or high school, I became aware of the many civic service clubs that existed in the Soo. Just about every town and village in our great country is blessed with these organizations. I recall my curiosity as to what the letters "BPOE" stood for as they pertained to the Elks Club. I asked an adult customer one day if he knew what those letters meant. He told me without hesitation, "Best People on Earth." I believed him for a long time; I was convinced this was so. I later learned, however, the acronym stood for "Benevolent Protective Order of the Elks."

As I reflect on the café's years of existence through trying and prosperous times, two major wars, recessions and the Depression, I truly believe that these letters and the initial interpretation I was told, "Best People on Earth," can include each and

139

every soul that stepped through the café doors. Whether they came to quench a thirst, to satisfy a hunger, to relax and chat, to meet a date, a spouse, a family member, create a business transaction, whatever the reason—they were the "Best People On Earth".

Old Age – Epilogue

The full impact of the term "old age" never really struck me until my knees began to "talk to me". When I consider the amount of standing, twisting, turning, kneeling and running up and down the basement stairs in the café several times a day for 43 years, it is not surprising that I would develop knee problems.

An old Greek saying, "We become what our fathers were," holds true in my case. When he was nearing 80, my father suffered with bad knees. Someone gave him a colorful cane from Mexico, which I inherited. It hid in a clothes closet for almost 40 years but became handy as I began to need it for the same purpose as my father—osteoarthritis of the knees.

All winter long, even before Christmas, a trip to the mailbox produced countless flower and vegetable seed catalogs. These would inspire my anticipation of the arrival of spring, the cleanup of winter's debris and the witness of the resurrection of God's earthly blessings. I loved planning, planting, tilling and pruning in my garden, but with the inability to kneel, gardening was not possible. I looked longingly at my vegetable garden one particular spring and my raised beds were choked with weeds. Normally, by this time of year, my garden beds were tilled and ready for planting.

Little did I realize that my inability to garden would depress me so deeply. That spring a good friend came to the rescue, tilling my garden, planting, weeding and harvesting. I was so grateful.

A salve to my gardening heartache came that year in a magazine column which caught my eye. The columnist ended his article with a quote that gave me a new perspective on my love and loss of gardening and reminded me of another satisfying passion, my love of books.

"Make books your companions; let your bookshelves be your gardens: Bask in their beauty, gather their fruit, pluck their roses, take their spices and myrrh. And when your soul be weary, change from garden to garden and from prospect to prospect."

– Judah Ben Saul (1120-1190).

Judah Ben Saul planted a seed, a seed which I have since nourished, exchanging some of the time I would have spent in my garden with time I now spend with books—delving into the pleasure of reading and enjoying the "ordering of the mind" that comes from writing. What a joy it has been "planning, planting, tilling and watering" this book. I have been blessed with an opportunity to write, and my life in the café, with the wonderful people of this town, is what I know best.

Acknowledgements

I am truly grateful to my wife Georgia for her love, patience, support and generosity of spirit and to our daughters Catherine, Joy and Anastasia for their encouragement, input and patience. Extra hugs to Cathie who took the time to go through four spiral notebooks, decipher my hand-written scribblings, organize the stories, type the manuscript and make the additions and changes with my constant revisions—all this squeezed in among her duties as wife, mother of two and the demands of her career. My sincere thanks also extend to:

- my sister Helen for her input on what she, sisters Sophie and Joy and brother, Sam, observed and experienced at The American Café during my service time in World War II;
- Leon Bennett, my Ashmun Street neighbor for many years, who took the time to read the manuscript and make suggestions as well as write a foreword for the book;
- Cris Roll and Deirdre Stevens who also read and edited the manuscript and provided reviews for the book;
- Jeffrey T. Rogg, Cathie's husband, for his review, helpful suggestions and thorough edits;
- my daughter Joy, for her very careful final read-through;
- my grandchildren: Pierce Telton Rogg, Blythe Georgiana Rogg, Christian David Harrison, Charlotte Irene Harrison, Hunter Knox Stacey and Hayden Fisher Stacey for their enthusiastic encouragement at the telling and retelling of the stories in this book;
- Sault Realism for expertise in copying and repairing the old photos, helping to preserve the past; and
- Sault Printing Company staff for their patience and guidance in this process, just as in years past when they printed the menus for The American Café.

In a few instances, names have been changed.